That I do not accept the faith that possessed [the Mormons] does not mean I doubt their . . . devotion and heroism. . . . Especially their women. Their women were incredible.

—*Wallace Stegner,* The Gathering of Zion: The Story of the Mormon Trail *(Lincoln: University of Nebraska Press, 1964), 13*

Getting Past the Labels

How the Truth Makes
Women Free

WENDY C. TOP

BOOKCRAFT
SALT LAKE CITY, UTAH

Library of Congress Cataloging-in-Publication Data

Top, Wendy C.
  Getting past the labels: how the truth makes women free/Wendy C. Top.
    p. cm.
  Includes bibliographical references.
  ISBN1-57345-624-1 (hardcover)
    1. Mormon women—Religious life. 2. Church of Jesus Christ of Latter-Day Saints—Doctrines. I. Title.
BX8641.T67 2000
248.8'43'088283—dc21

                                             99-086518

Printed in the United States of America   18961-6625

10 9 8 7 6 5 4 3 2 1

2-14-2004
Happy Valentine Day,
Love,
Steven

To my daughters,

Jessica, Tiffany, and Emma Jane

Contents

Preface

This book is almost unrecognizable from the first draft. Both the manuscript and I have undergone a substantial metamorphosis in the protracted and sometimes painful process of bringing it to fruition. I know that any inspiration I may have received was not because anyone needed to read this book, but because I needed to write it. I am a different person from when I started it.

I am deeply indebted to many women who have reviewed my manuscript in its various forms over the last four or five years. Their suggestions have been valuable and sometimes eye-opening. I fear that if I start listing names I will leave someone out, but I do want to express special thanks to Sheri Dew, Emily Watts, and especially Suzanne Brady at Deseret Book for seeing potential in my first manuscript, but also for not allowing me to stop there. As I struggled to catch their vision of what women needed and what the book could be, it raised my sights to an even nobler and more complete understanding of the role of all women, not just those who were like me. I have glimpsed the potential of the sisters of the Church, and my love for them and my gratitude at being one of them have grown accordingly. It is my hope, through the personal odyssey that has become this book, to inspire and expand their perceptions of themselves as daughters of God to heights and depths and breadths they may never have considered.

The Lies 1 That Bind

One evening, while watching our daughters play a Young Women's basketball game, a friend mentioned to me that her older daughter who was away at college was struggling with the question of why women could not hold the priesthood. "There is nothing wrong with asking that question," declared my concerned friend, "but she is asking the wrong people!"

Her statement led me back in my mind over the years to the time when *I* was searching for the answer to that sometimes prickly question. I remembered the day in the late 1970s or early 1980s when I watched Barbara B. Smith, then general president of the Relief Society, on Phil Donahue's daytime talk show, explaining and defending the Church's stand against the Equal Rights Amendment. I felt incensed at the attacks that were being made against the Church, and from that came a growing desire to proclaim that faithful Latter-day Saint women *should be* the most truly liberated women in the world. I felt that was true at the time even though I did not yet fully understand how that concept fit in with the patriarchal order, why women didn't hold priesthood, and furthermore why I didn't always feel that way in actual practice. I only knew that the Church, doctrinally and institutionally, venerated and respected women and that it was the only religion I knew that taught of a Mother in Heaven as well as a Father in Heaven and held out the promise of godhood to all faithful members, men and women.

As I spoke with my friend about her daughter, I realized that when I asked why women couldn't hold the priesthood, it was not really because I was agitating to be a bishop or a stake president, or to baptize my children. What I was really asking was, "Am I of equal worth with men even though I don't hold the priesthood?" "Does my obligation to follow the men who hold the priesthood mean I am less valuable or capable than they are?" and "If I am fully equal to men, how do I make an equal contribution when I cannot do all that a priesthood holder does, or when I must make my contribution behind the scenes?"

I have pursued this question not because the world says I should demand every privilege a man has. Rather, having faith that the teachings of the gospel are true and the Church is organized according to the Lord's will, I know that I need not be afraid to ask the Lord any honest question. I have been searching, collecting, and pondering answers for many years.

Just when I thought I had finally pulled it all together, I found that I still had a lot left to learn and other equally important related issues to confront. I thought that in addressing this question of why women don't hold the priesthood, I might make a few men in the Church uneasy.

However, I have discovered that it is the women of the Church who tend to be the most insecure about their roles, and that the priesthood question is only the beginning.

Equal with Each Other

In the course of a discussion with three women, I complained that because I had married and had a family and had not finished my college degree, many people automatically assumed I was stupid. Some seemed to imply, "What's wrong with you—why don't you have any ambition?" One of the other women, about my age and not yet married, asserted that for every time I had been criticized for giving up my education for marriage, she had been needled for being single and having a career. "What's wrong with you—why aren't you married and having a family?" As the conversation went on, I discovered that another of the women was a working mother, and in my mind I could hear people saying to her, "What's wrong with you—why aren't you home with your children?" And then I remembered the women I had known who were married but didn't have children, and how I'd overheard others say, "What's wrong with her—how can she be so selfish?" I suddenly realized what a minefield modern women have to negotiate all through their lives. While we have many more possibilities today, we also have many more landmines and pitfalls. Women perform in combat every day!

Unfortunately, as women, sometimes we are each other's worst enemies instead of the supportive network of daughters of God that we ought to be. The more I talked with these women, the more I realized how unsure we were of ourselves and how each of us wanted her role validated, perhaps even somewhat at the expense of other roles. A light went on in my head: *Women not only want to be of equal worth with men, they want to be of equal worth with each other!*

A few days later, I recognized this insecurity again in myself when searching for a story I had heard told by a woman speaker at a BYU devotional assembly. As I read the words of the introduction of the speaker, I recalled the momentary resentment I had felt when I had heard all of her many professional accomplishments trumpeted from the podium. She also had several children and mentioned in passing something in her talk about having left them in a day-care center at one time, though how often and for how long, I had no idea. I remembered saying to myself that I could have accomplished the things she had, but I was willing to sacrifice my own selfish attainments for husband and family. However, after the revealing conversation I'd had with the three women editors, as I reread that introduction I finally had to admit what I had known in the back of my mind all along: I had never had any desire to accomplish professionally outside my home. I was doing exactly what I had always wanted to do and what I felt I was foreordained to do, and I had to allow the same possibility for her. And yet, because I struggled with feeling inferior to her, I wanted to make her wrong.

Somehow I and all the women of the Church have got to find the courage to forget about everyone else's choices and pursue our own paths and fulfill our own missions. We have got to get past the labels *married, single, mother, childless, professional, homemaker,* and any other pigeon-holing definition and see ourselves first and foremost as daughters of God, each with her own equally important mission and unique powers and abilities.

I was beginning to catch on to this concept when, a few days after the incident mentioned above, I was called by a young woman who was editing an article I had written. Someone had put some things in my biographical information that were incorrect, and others that were an exaggeration to make me sound more interesting and accomplished than I was. I was frustrated that being a wife, mother, and homemaker was not considered enough, especially to an LDS audience. I asked the editor to change the information and put in the "wife, mother, home-maker" bit. She agreed and brightly chimed that, after all, that was the most important job of all. After what I'd been learning, I added, "If that is your mission in life."

Bound by the Lies of Satan

Because I see myself and many of my sisters in the Church frequently laboring under these unnecessary mental burdens, I have reached a point of rebellion. I am boldly advocating a women's liberation movement within the Church. I don't mean this in the stereotypical "women's movement" sense of the past three decades; I am talking about the ultimate liberation—the truth that will free us from the destructive, diabolical chains that Satan cleverly winds around us as he subtly whispers his lies about womanhood in our ears. Although the women's movement has been a blessing in many ways—to the extent that it has brought about truth—it has put an even greater burden on us in others. Even as we have gained more physical and social opportunities, we are more spiritually and emotionally enslaved than ever in other arenas. Why? Because Satan has cleverly switched one form of oppression—the undervaluing of women by men—for another and perhaps more devastating form—the undervaluing of women by themselves.

Pushing us to compare ourselves to each other or to an impossible ideal is a brilliant satanic tactic. Most faithful women are not likely to fall prey to the ordinary, workaday sins that seemingly trip up the rest of the world with ease. Satan knows that their weakness is not that they are not trying hard enough but that they are trying too hard. He has learned how to turn this to his advantage. He is experienced enough to know that negative thoughts will make us just as miserable as sinful ones and will just as effectively keep us from finding out who we really are. "He who in the first estate was thrust down delights in having us put ourselves down," cautioned Elder Neal A. Maxwell. "Self-contempt is of Satan; there is none of it in heaven" (*Notwithstanding My Weakness* [Salt Lake City: Deseret Book, 1981], 10). As Latter-day Saint women, we need to break free of the enslaving falsehoods engendered by the pressures we put on ourselves and each other to measure up to an unrealistic standard.

The Philosophies of the World

The philosophies of the world lie to us by relentlessly sending the message that we are not equal to men unless we are exactly like them, claiming all the same power, privileges, and recognition even if that means adopting their roles and behaviors and abandoning our own. The most outspoken feminists have, for decades, made the mistake of defining *equality* as *sameness*—women should be treated in *exactly* the same way as men are—relentlessly intimidating government, churches, and society to accept that definition. The word *feminists,* at least in this case, is an ironic misnomer. Many feminists haven't promoted femininity at all, but would more appropriately be called *masculinists,* because they continually and almost ruthlessly at times demand that women be treated exactly like men (even if that actually requires "special" treatment). And in order to gain this equal treatment, they have supposed that they must become just like men, betraying their own feminine gifts and power. In so doing, they have unwittingly admitted that being a woman is not good enough. This message subtly but persistently chips away at our vision of ourselves as women.

The world would further cajole us into believing that we are wasting our lives if we stay behind the scenes and sacrifice the accolades and rewards of society for the betterment of its people. Like the carrot in front of the rabbit, Satan and the worldly who do his bidding relentlessly taunt us with the mirage of the woman, wife, and mother who can have it all—career, marriage, family, sexuality, self-fulfillment—and sacrifice nothing. The social pressure to be successful in worldly terms is overbearing at times. One friend of mine spoke of the alluring voices persuading her that she was wasting her college education at home; she wondered why there didn't seem to be more fulfillment in motherhood. Another struggled because she had been convinced that the contribution she was making at her job would have a greater impact on the betterment of the world than being home to raise her small children. As committed as I have tried to be to putting my wife and mother roles first, I have sometimes felt a temptation to prove myself to the world by satisfying its definition of success and self-worth.

To make the obsession doubly exhausting and impossible, "they" (who are "they"? They are Satan!) persist in selling us also the fantasy of the one perfect female body. Lucifer is without scruples or mercy. Anything short of perfection in any area is failure; few variations in body type are acceptable. The worst part of it all is that even LDS women, we who should know who we really are, buy into these ridiculous myths. Before we came to earth, we were anxious to have a body of any kind. We understood what a transcendent gift it would be to have a body, even if it were not perfect. Now that we are here, many of us hate and berate our bodies when they deserve and need to be loved, respected, and cared for just as our spirits do, no matter what their condition. Such negative attitudes can't help but take a toll on both body *and* spirit.

I continually have to fight to keep myself from believing Satan's perfect-body myth. I have likewise watched all three of my daughters, like so many young women today, obsess about their bodies. I have seen them go up and down emotionally, losing confidence in themselves as they put on weight and regaining confidence as they take it off. I have watched them starve themselves and then—famished, defeated, and seeking comfort and reassurance—stuff themselves with food. Horrified at their own lack of self-discipline, they compulsively exercise for three or four hours to make up for it.

This battle with the body is symbolic and symptomatic of the battle with the myth of the woman who can do it all. Obviously, another clever by-product of Satan's merciless promotion of comparison and self-contempt is the fact that it causes us to be inordinately preoccupied with ourselves. Besides the terrible physical and emotional damage this does to women's lives, I believe it does great spiritual damage as well. We are so absorbed in ourselves—how we look and what we need and whether or not other people like us or think we are attractive or capable—that we have little time and energy to think about and serve others or to seek God's will instead of our own.

True self-confidence does not come in obsessing over ourselves, whether out of insecurity or even vanity, but in losing ourselves completely in the soul-building service of God. Lasting self-security comes not in what we make of ourselves but in what God makes of us. Only he can give us the true gifts of self-love (the pure love of Christ) and inner peace. Caught between the blatant enticing of the world and the gentle whisperings of the Spirit, we may languish and waste our time and potential in guilt and uncertainty, never discovering our real power or accomplishing the great missions God has planned for us individually. If we fall prey to these philosophies, we are just as oppressed and underestimated by society as women who were once falsely considered to be second-class citizens incapable of the same privileges and responsibilities as men.

Self-Imposed Ideals

For a time, I paid a high and ongoing price in the form of clinical depression for trying to match up to the mirage of "Molly Mormon/Patty Perfect." I spent many years trying to do every good thing I saw in others (sometimes resenting them for it) or heard about at church or read about in the *Ensign*. For instance, I would see Sister A with all her lovely children and think, "I should be having more children. I am supposed to have a lot of children like Sister A." I would hear in Relief Society about how everyone loved Sister B because she was always the first person to bring in a meal or give a baby shower, and I would think how selfish I was with my time and how I should be more like Sister B. In sacrament meeting I heard Sister C say that her family had never missed a family home evening, and I felt unworthy because we missed quite regularly. I fretted that my husband and I should be as faithful as Sister C and her husband. I often mistook well-intentioned Mormon traditions for carved-in-stone commandments. I got caught on the treadmill of trying to do everything I was ever asked to do in the Church, being concerned about what others might think if my children didn't earn their awards, causing strife in my marriage because my husband drank Coke. The list could go on. I tried to do what I thought others expected of me and what I expected of myself. It never occurred to me to ask the Lord what He expected of me. I just assumed that if it was taught in the Church, or if other LDS sisters were doing it, it was part of the gospel, and I had to do it. When I finally crashed and reached the point that I could barely do anything, I figured out that I simply could not do or be all good things at once. I had to stop looking outward to find out what path to pursue; instead I began turning inward, not to my own will or desires but to God's. Anything else was futile and only led to more unhappiness.

When we put unrealistic demands on ourselves, sometimes our next step is to extend those demands to our sisters. Do we measure each other's faithfulness by our own impossible yardsticks? Perhaps in our perfectionism we feel pressured to judge, label, and condemn others, holding the mistaken impression that this will make us feel better about ourselves (which it might, for a nanosecond). If we can discredit a sister, we can discredit her talents and accomplishments and therefore not feel as threatened by them or as pressured to imitate them.

A close friend of mine once observed, "Men compete and women compare." Men feel they must *beat* each other at everything, and women feel they must *be* each other in everything! Comparing or competing is always a lose/lose exercise. We will feel either superior or inferior, neither of which is a righteous or helpful outcome. Sister Patricia

Holland pointed this out as one of the unwelcome side effects of the diversity of modern life for women:

> Because of [this diversity] we seem even more uncertain and less secure with each other. We are getting not closer but further away from that sense of community and sisterhood that has sustained us and given us unique strength for generations. There seems to be an increase in our competitiveness and a decrease in our generosity with one another. . . . We must not feel so frightened; we must not be so threatened and insecure; we must not need to find exact replicas of ourselves in order to feel validated as women of worth. ("Many Things . . . One Thing," in *A Heritage of Faith* [Salt Lake City: Deseret Book, 1988], 15–16)

Do we have any idea how much we are holding ourselves, each other, and the Church back when we wittingly or unwittingly cling to some well-intentioned but impossible ideal? We are all going to go down together!

Sisters, Unite!

It seems that most of us labor at least occasionally under these unnecessary burdens and mistaken ideas, though we seldom admit it. Whenever I speak on these subjects, I receive an overwhelming response from women *and* men who are grateful for my willingness to speak honestly and openly about the secret battle in which so many of us are engaged and which is threatening to overwhelm us. I hope in the following chapters of this book to deal with these issues that I believe trip LDS women up the most—including some issues with men and priesthood—and then to help each woman discover and appreciate the powerful influence she can have on those around her if she cultivates her own talents and gifts.

Let us, therefore, stand united and declare ourselves freed from the lies and deceptions of Satan in order that we may be effectual instruments in the hand of God. The battle will be unrelenting because the forces arrayed against us will never give up trying to render us feeble and useless. Satan's tactic is to "wear out the saints of the most High" (Daniel 7:25) by confronting them unceasingly with diabolical, almost irresistible falsehoods. But if we choose we can arm ourselves with the most discerning, powerful weapon in all eternity—the Lord's invincible sword of truth. Indeed, "[We] shall know the truth, and the truth shall make [us] free" (John 8:32)!

The Truth Shall Make You Free

There seems to me to be no limit to what a righteous woman can accomplish, especially when she works with truth—God's truth—instead of the enslaving lies of Satan or the misleading philosophies of the world. I fully believe that we can lift not only ourselves and our families but also the Church and the rest of the world to new heights when we fully comprehend what it means to be daughters of Deity.

In order to fill the measure of our unique creation as women, we must learn to see ourselves as royal daughters of heavenly parents and as equal and complementary partners not only with our brothers but also with each other. I have come to understand that as I speak about women working side by side with priesthood holders, I must emphasize over and over again that I am not referring only to the formal roles of wife and mother. First and foremost I am speaking of daughters of God who accomplished great things in the premortal existence, where they were neither wives nor mothers, and who still have many imperative missions to fill on this earth in cooperation with sons of God who hold the priesthood. I am further suggesting that we complement instead of compete with each other, both men and women. Just as women can do many things that men can't, and vice versa, single or childless women can do many things that wives and mothers can't, and vice versa. Working mothers and widowed or divorced women can make equally important contributions that may be impossible for others. Individually, each woman has something to contribute that another doesn't. When speaking of the various spiritual gifts given to different individuals, Paul used this powerfully convincing image of the body of Christ to teach the Corinthians the absolute importance of each member:

> For as the body is one, and hath many members, and all the members of that one body, being many, are one body: so also is Christ.
>
> For by one Spirit are we all baptized into one body, whether we be Jews or Gentiles [men or women], whether we be bond or free [married or single, parents or childless]; and have been all made to drink into one Spirit.
>
> For the body is not one member, but many.
>
> If the foot shall say, Because I am not the hand, I am not of the body; is it therefore not of the body?
>
> And if the ear shall say, Because I am not the eye, I am not of the body; is it therefore not of the body?

If the whole body were an eye, where were the hearing? If the whole were hearing, where were the smelling?

But now hath God set the members every one of them in the body, as it hath pleased him.

And if they were all one member, where were the body?

But now are they many members, yet but one body.

And the eye cannot say unto the hand, I have no need of thee: nor again the head to the feet, I have no need of you.

Nay, much more those members of the body, which seem to be more feeble, are necessary:

And those members of the body, which we think to be less honourable, upon these we bestow more abundant honour; and our uncomely parts have more abundant comeliness.

For our comely parts have no need: but God hath tempered the body together, having given more abundant honour to that part which lacked:

That there should be no schism in the body; but that the members should have the same care one for another.

And whether one member suffer, all the members suffer with it; or one member be honoured, all the members rejoice with it.

Now ye are the body of Christ, and members in particular. (1 Corinthians 12:12–27)

In this metaphor, Paul skillfully implies we should be grateful for our differences. Together we make up the body of Christ, and it works most effectively when each member does his or her part instead of working against or trying to imitate or replace the others. If we were all the same, most of us wouldn't be needed! There is an indispensable role for *every* daughter of God to fill on this earth, no matter how visible or invisible, traditional or nontraditional it may be. For instance, I would never want a daughter of mine or any other woman who did not marry and/or have children in mortality to go through life thinking she never did the really important stuff. In God's economy, all divinely ordained missions are of equal value because all souls are of equal value, no matter how different they may be. As sisters, we must support and not judge each other, even when we think mistakes are being made. We are all going to make mistakes in searching out our roles, but we can find the right way more quickly with loving support than through criticism and condemnation.

Equally Valued Roles

In connection with this truth, I would hate to see any woman go through life feeling that there must be something deficient in her because she doesn't fill traditional roles. I can understand the tendency of single women, for instance, to continually ask, "What is wrong with me; why am I not married?" I have discovered that this may be a pointless question. Though I am married now, I did get a taste of the loneliness of not dating and continually blaming something in myself for it. I had dated quite a lot in high school, but when I went to BYU I hardly had a date my entire freshman year. It was especially hard on me because I measured my self-esteem by the amount of male attention I received. All year long I agonized over why I was so unappealing to everyone but the very boys I couldn't stand. By the end of the year, I was relieved to go home and escape the social dating pressure, burying my self-doubt in long workdays at my job.

Just two months later, my future husband returned from his mission and started dating me almost every night. It wasn't until long after we were married that I realized that the painful year I had spent not dating at BYU was the very experience that deepened and matured me and prepared me to meet and marry my husband. I'd had to reach deep within and learn to find strength and happiness in more meaningful and eternal things than dating and male attention. Had I not been forced to stretch so far, I would have remained the same shallow little teenybopper I had been in high school, and my husband might have passed me by. It wasn't that there was something wrong with me. It was the fulfilling of the Lord's plan for me. He had something even more important for me to learn and do.

It is my feeling that if a woman has done all she can and remains single or childless, it is useless, self-defeating, even wasteful to ask, "What is wrong with me?" A better question might be, "What am I to learn from this, and what am I to do with it?" As sisters and supporters of each other, we also have to get past the idea that there must be something wrong with a woman who doesn't fit the standard mold. I have an unmarried friend who is not much younger than I am, and I often find myself thinking, "If only she weren't so independent!" Who am I to say this is a problem? As a single woman, she has the flexibility to serve in ways that are different from my ways. Are they not just as acceptable to the Lord?

One of my favorite heroines from history is a great example of this. Corrie ten Boom was a Christian woman who, with her cherished sister Betsie, was incarcerated in a Nazi concentration camp as punishment for hiding Jews in their home. She later wrote books and traveled the world to bear witness of how her faith in Christ helped her overcome all the trials of her life.

Corrie had been deeply in love when she was a young woman. Though she was loved in return, her young man married another woman who was more acceptable to his family because she had more money and social status than Corrie. Corrie was devastated as he introduced his new wife to her and expressed the hope that the two women could be friends. Later, weeping bitterly in her room, Corrie heard her Papa's footsteps on the stairs as he came up to console her. She dreaded hearing him say that there would soon be someone else, for somehow she knew deep in her heart that there never would be. Instead, her dear Papa gave her this sage counsel: "There are two things we can do when this happens. We can kill the love so that it stops hurting. But then of course part of us dies, too. Or, Corrie, we can ask God to open up another route for that love to travel" (*The Hiding Place* [New York: Bantam Books, 1971], 44).

So Corrie consciously pleaded with God to help her

take her love for that young man and channel it to Jesus Christ, to let him take charge of her life. Years later, while visiting with a fellow woman missionary who was very bitter about never having married, she related how she further came to grips with her own situation. She explained, "If [we] reach out and take someone for [ourselves] and the Lord steps in between . . . it means He is protecting us from someone we should not have because He has a far greater purpose for our lives. . . . There are some, like me, who are called to live a single life. . . . Others . . . are called to prepare for marriage which may come later in life. They, too, are blessed, for God is using the in-between years to teach them that marriage is not the answer to unhappiness. Happiness is found only in a balanced relationship with the Lord Jesus" (*Tramp for the Lord* [New York: Jove Books, 1974], 158–59).

The Innate Motherhood of All Women

Having said this about the equally valuable roles of women, I have to draw a bottom line. Eternally speaking, the roles of wife and mother are ultimately the most important. If that were not true, we would all be perfectly happy in the terrestrial kingdom. Because we are daughters of heavenly parents, all women are genetically programmed, spiritually speaking, to become heavenly wives and mothers. That is why I believe all women are mothers even now—have all the gifts and abilities of mothering, even though those attributes may not be used in physical motherhood during mortality.

I like to compare the many uses of the motherhood

qualities of all women to the multiple uses of seeds. All the seeds my husband lovingly plants in his beloved garden each spring contain the potential to germinate, blossom, produce fruit, and thus reproduce themselves, but not all do. Yet, no matter what, they can still be useful. Sometimes in his concern for the tiny carrot seeds, for example, he overwaters them, and they decompose before sprouting, but in doing so they return nourishment to the soil. In the autumn we like to take the seeds from inside our Halloween pumpkins, season them, roast them in the oven, and then eat them. Seeds that we start in containers and eat as sprouts are especially healthy. None of these ever get the chance to reproduce, but they are a highly nutritious and tasty food source. More often than we would like, some of the seeds we plant in our garden are eaten by birds that may carry them to faraway lands where they are passed out whole and take root and grow, perhaps bringing new beauty and fertility to barren soils. Finally, we keep many seeds stored and saved in our food storage as security against an uncertain future. They must wait to fulfill the measure of their creation, but what a source of peace and comfort they are to us in the meantime. If we ever do have to use them when we are desperate for food, how much more they will be appreciated than the seeds that produce in times of plenty.

Likewise, I believe all women inherently have attributes and capabilities of motherhood that may be applied to improving the world and furthering Heavenly Father's plans in many different ways. That overused saying "God could not be everywhere, so he made mothers" applies to all righteous women, not just those who bear children. Indeed, President Gordon B. Hinckley has spoken of women as the crowning achievement or "masterpiece" of God's creations (see "Daughters of God," *Ensign*, November 1991, 99). Speaking of the mothering capabilities inherent in all women regardless of their situation, Sister Patricia Holland emphasized that we must work together: "Whatever our circumstance, we can reach out, touch, hold, lift, and nurture—but we cannot do it in isolation. We need a community of sisters stilling the soul and binding the wounds of fragmentation" ("Many Things . . . One Thing," in *A Heritage of Faith* [Salt Lake City: Deseret Book, 1988], 27).

If we can make this unity a reality, I believe that the women of the Church are on the verge of a new era of unprecedented opportunities for both personal and institutional growth and accomplishment. However, we will never fully realize this great new awakening until we fully awaken and determine to become all that we can be in the Lord's hands. Though it applies specifically to Jerusalem and the Jews, I believe the following scripture could be echoed as a call to the women of Zion: "Awake, and arise from the dust, . . . put on thy beautiful garments, O daughter of Zion; and strengthen thy stakes and enlarge thy borders forever, that thou mayest no more be confounded, that the covenants of the Eternal Father which he hath made unto thee, . . . may be fulfilled" (Moroni 10:31).

Becoming Free in Christ

How do we find the power to free ourselves from the captivity of our own distorted thinking? How do we learn to feel valuable in our uniqueness as well as in the things that bind us together? How do we join together to become the powerful, united force that we are capable of becoming? The only infallible answer lies in Jesus Christ.

To begin with, we must each stay safely within the framework of a faithful Latter-day Saint. Yet, within that framework there is still vast room for individual expression, even when it may seem to be going against the common grain. We should encourage rather than judge each other. Elder B. H. Roberts captured this sentiment succinctly when he advised, "In essentials let there be unity; in nonessentials, liberty; and in all things, charity" (as quoted in D. Kelly Ogden and Andrew C. Skinner, *New Testament Apostles Testify of Christ* [Salt Lake City: Deseret Book, 1998], 148). The ultimate test of the correctness of a woman's course in the world is not the prevailing public opinions of the Church membership but the private approbation of our Heavenly Father and the Lord Jesus Christ. In the end nothing else matters—neither the opinions of the world nor the judgments of other sisters nor even our own opinions of ourselves. I have discovered that when I seek God's will and God's approval only, I feel safe and confident with myself. When the Spirit of the Lord is with me, I am whole and complete. I can look at other sisters who seem more talented or who have pursued a different path and feel that I am equally valuable. I can glory in their successes as well as my own.

I have come to believe that this focusing on Jesus Christ and seeking the guidance of his Spirit is the "one thing . . . needful" that the Lord himself taught women to pursue, as opposed to the "many things" about which we are so often "careful and troubled." The Lord gave this counsel directly to two women whom he dearly loved and in whose home he often spent time. It is noteworthy to women that this incident is included in the scriptures:

> Now it came to pass, as they went, that he entered into a certain village: and a certain woman named Martha received him into her house.
>
> And she had a sister called Mary, which also sat at Jesus' feet, and heard his word.
>
> But Martha was cumbered about much serving, and came to him, and said, Lord, dost thou not care that my sister hath left me to serve alone? bid her therefore that she help me.
>
> And Jesus answered and said unto her, Martha, Martha, thou art careful and troubled about many things:
>
> But one thing is needful: and Mary hath chosen that good part, which shall not be taken away from her. (Luke 10:38–42)

Most women are quite familiar with this story and the gentle charge given to Martha as she complained to Jesus that Mary would not help with the traditional work of the women. Yet if most women are like me, they have struggled over the ultimate meaning of his reply.

Some have used this scripture as an excuse for not attending to duties in the home. In fact, it is often mis-quoted as saying that "Mary hath chosen the *better* part." Note that the Lord does not make a direct comparison between the two women. Martha evidently means well in believing that she as a woman must keep up the traditions and expectations of her culture in preparing an elaborate meal for her guests. Her frustration comes through in her comment to Jesus, *"dost thou not care* that my sister hath left me to serve alone." I don't fault Martha for this; I recognize these same feelings and behaviors in myself when I am overwhelmed and frustrated in trying to do what *I* think is right.

Rather than take it personally, Jesus kindly chides Martha, pointing out that *at this particular time,* "one thing is needful," at least for Mary, and by implication perhaps for Martha also. Generally speaking, we know that our own relationship with the Lord is more important than anything else, but certainly not to the continual exclusion or neglect of making a comfortable and happy home for our loved ones. Indeed, no matter how much spiritual knowledge we may gain, we will never be exalted without service, and yet, there is a right or best time for everything. We must find balance in life so that we will focus on the right thing at the right time—something we can do only with the guidance of the Holy Spirit. Whereas the "one thing needful" in this instance may have been taking the opportunity to be taught at the feet of the Lord, the "one thing needful" in another instance may have been feeding the hungry.

The "one thing needful" in every instance is to focus on Christ and do his will for us at that time. For this reason, we must respect others enough to let them make choices according to their own missions in life. Similarly, we must have the courage to follow our own path where the Spirit leads us, no matter how much it differs from that of other women or from the traditions or expectations of the culture. Again, we will see mistakes in this process, both in our own lives and in the lives of our sisters, but with loving support, these can be corrected much more quickly than with criticism and judgment. I find it fascinating that John, recording a later incident at the home of Martha and Mary during the week before Christ's death, makes a point of mentioning that Mary anointed the feet of Christ with costly oil and wiped them with her hair, and as for Martha, "they made him a supper; and Martha served" (John 12:2). Apparently, through listening to the voice of the Lord, Martha had found peace in her role and had learned to respect Mary's as well, for both centered on service to Christ.

The Study of Behavior Will Not Free Us

One problem we have is that sometimes, instead of focusing on the voice of the Lord, we buy into other gimmicks, even in the Church. The world has developed all kinds of therapeutic methods and positive-thinking tricks to help us like ourselves. In my family, when someone is feeling picked on, we jokingly repeat the self-affirmations we once heard made fun of on television: "I'm smart enough and I'm good enough and, doggonnit! People like me!" Even when we are serious, these statements are sometimes helpful, but I believe they are limited in their effect. Over the years I have repeatedly discovered the truth of Elder Boyd K. Packer's maxim: "True doctrine, understood, changes attitudes and behavior. The study of the doctrines of the gospel will improve behavior quicker than a study of behavior will improve behavior" (Conference Report, October 1986, 20).

I sometimes wonder if part of the reason women in the Church feel such pressure to conform to a preconceived mold or to continually compare their behavior to that of other women is because much of our time in lessons and meetings is spent discussing behavior instead of doctrine. Sometimes we spend so much time offering our own ideas and opinions about what a principle means or how it is to be lived—what I call gospel chit-chat—that the teacher is unable to present the doctrine! For instance, I once heard a discussion that was supposed to focus on the crowning doctrine of charity devolve into a discussion about writing thank-you notes and giving baby showers. More than once I have watched a lesson on spiritual and temporal self-reliance boil down to a drawn-out discussion on food storage in which someone inevitably reminds the sisters that if they aren't using their food storage now, they won't know how to use it when they need it. This, in turn, leads to concern over the number of women in the ward who don't know how to make bread from scratch. Thus, instead of general principles of application, such an undirected exchange often focuses on outward behavior that may, for some sisters, set up a seemingly impossible standard—and not one that is necessarily required by the Lord.

In a Relief Society lesson in my friend's ward, a question from a teacher on how we can teach our children modesty once elicited the enthusiastic response from a sister that she never allowed her children to wear shorts or sleeveless shirts because when they began to wear garments, they would not be able to wear such clothes. My friend felt like crawling under her seat. She had never even thought of such a thing! She knew that everyone there was aware that her kids often ran around the neighborhood in their swimsuits all day. And I must admit that I have never been very good at writing thank-you notes or giving baby showers, and I haven't made bread from scratch for more than twenty years. So although sharing specific ideas has some merit, we need to proceed with caution, not confusing household hints with gospel doctrine. We should recognize that for some struggling, often insecure sisters who are trying to fit that imaginary mold of the perfect LDS woman, such a discussion can be discouraging. It just gives them more "shoulds" to add to their list and more voices that taunt in their heads. I know that we mean well, but I think it may be time to reevaluate the messages we send each other as sisters about how a Latter-day Saint woman must perform.

Further, we often make ourselves and each other crazy by the many frilly, frothy, traditional but unnecessary behaviors we expect of ourselves. Notice that men never seem to go overboard on details the way we do. Have you ever seen a man teach a lesson with a centerpiece? or hand out a bookmark with a ribbon and a quote from the lesson? When men are in charge of refreshments, are the treats nutritionally well balanced and color coordinated? Are they all homemade? Are they presented in colorful, fabric-lined baskets? I'm not saying these things aren't nice and even uplifting sometimes, but when they become the primary focus, cause undue stress, or are a substitute for the more important, life-changing things we are supposed to be doing in the Church, we are wasting our time, power, and effectiveness.

I remember a year when my husband and I were in charge of the ward Christmas party. We planned several things to try to make the event meaningful and eliminate some of the chaos created by excited and sometimes unsupervised children. Overall, the party was a great success, but I had so exhausted myself physically and emotionally in preparing all the superficial aspects that I could not enjoy it. In fact, I cried for several days afterward because the details had not gone precisely according to plan. The food line had moved too slowly, and some of the games hadn't worked very well, and therefore the children were still running helter-skelter through the building. My husband was quite pleased with the activity, but I was in mourning because it hadn't lived up to my hyper-expectations. Never mind the fact that the food was a huge hit, or that we started a tradition of writing to the missionaries at the ward Christmas party that continues in that ward today—I was too stressed to see anything good coming from it or to feel the Christmas spirit in the fellowship of ward members.

I have noticed that this tendency to overdo things is often an occupational hazard of womanhood. Our sensitivity to detail can, when held in balance, beautify and soften the world, but when it gets out of balance it can have just the opposite effect. We can actually make ourselves and everyone around us crazy! We lose what we sought to gain and "spend . . . [our] labor for that which cannot satisfy" (2 Nephi 9:51).

Returning to the story of Mary and Martha, I discovered an interesting interpretation in some Bible commentaries. Several scholars have explained that the ancient meaning of the word translated as *thing* was *dish*. In this interpretation, Christ was saying that only one simple dish was necessary to feed him and his disciples, rather than the elaborate feast Martha felt driven to prepare. This was not a time to worry about traditions and outward performances; it was a time to keep the preparations simple so that Martha and all the others could feast on the words of Jesus Christ. Indeed, when Christ spoke of "one dish," his words carried a double meaning. He was reminding Martha that *he* was the one dish needful that, unlike food that would be gobbled up and gone within a day, would never be taken away from her and Mary. He is the answer to our spiritual and emotional malnutrition.

Following are five ways in which we can "Come unto the Holy One of Israel, and feast upon that which perisheth not, neither can be corrupted, and let [our] soul[s] delight in fatness" (2 Nephi 9:51):

1. *Learn and teach the doctrines of Christ.* If the overemphasis on behavior is indeed putting pressure on LDS women to conform to one single mold, perhaps we could progress faster if we would heed Elder Packer's words and be sure that we emphasize doctrine—especially the doctrine of Christ and his perfect love for us. I have found

that the love of Christ is the ultimate motivator. Then, as we speak briefly about application, we should encourage each other to seek the guidance of the Lord through his Spirit in applying that doctrine to our own lives individually. Any given doctrine might offer something quite different for each sister according to her circumstances and abilities. Learning, understanding, and gaining a witness of the doctrine taught will be a far greater motivation to change and can perhaps then be enhanced by the inspired opinions and ideas of other sisters.

My favorite example of changing behavior through teaching doctrine is found in the Book of Mormon. When Alma the Younger discovers that his son Corianton has committed adultery, how does he deal with him? He does not conduct a discussion of ideas on "How can we stay morally clean?" or give Corianton a quote to put on his refrigerator that reminds him to think clean thoughts! As recorded in chapters 39–42 of Alma, he mentions only briefly the adultery (though emphasizing its seriousness) but then takes great pains to explain to his son the atonement of Christ—the plan of salvation and the doctrine of restoration. He knew from his previous experience that the word of God "had more powerful effect upon the minds of the people than . . . anything else, which had happened unto them—therefore Alma thought it was expedient that [he] should try the virtue of the word of God" (Alma 31:5). I am likewise convinced that the only way we will ever completely escape our self-defeating behaviors—or truly change any kind of negative behavior, for that matter—is by immersing ourselves in the pure doctrines of Christ through the holy scriptures, the words of the living prophets, and the teachings of the temple, coupled with fasting and prayer.

Consider another example. Suppose a lesson on charity were focused first and foremost on exploring the doctrine of charity. The scriptures have a lot to say on this most important subject. In fact, we would learn that charity *is* the most important subject. It is not just service or love, but "the pure love of Christ" (Moroni 7:47). We would learn that even if we possessed all other spiritual gifts and could heal, speak in tongues, or even move mountains, if we didn't have charity, we would still be nothing and our gifts would be of no avail. If we took casseroles to every woman in the world every night and wrote thank-you notes until our fingers dropped off, or even gave all our money to the poor, but didn't have charity, it would mean nothing (see 1 Corinthians 13:1–3).

We would come to understand that charity is the whole purpose of our existence. All of the commandments are given to lead us to have charity—love for God and our fellowmen (see 1 Timothy 1:5; Mark 12:30–31). The only way we can be like Christ is to be filled with charity, or love, because God *is* love (see 1 John 4:8; Moroni 7:47–48). We could read about all the manifestations of charity—that it suffers long and is not puffed up, that it is not selfish and never fails (see 1 Corinthians 13:4–8). We would learn that we don't obtain charity simply by working harder, serving more, and being nicer—though we must be willing to do these things as directed by the Spirit—but that it is a spiritual gift bestowed by God upon true followers of Christ who pray with all the energy of their hearts that they might be filled with it (see Moroni 7:48). True love, service, and all the other attributes of charity, then, are the natural result of receiving this gift, not characteristics we create in ourselves.

The more we learn, the more we will come to know Christ, become like him, and understand that charity is a deep and eternal doctrine that cannot be encapsulated in discussions of outward behaviors that may or may not reflect charity. A lesson focused on that true doctrine would leave us not with more obligations and lists of things to *do* (or at least feel guilty about not doing), but with a love of Christ and a vision of who we want to *be*. Hopefully, we would be filled with the Spirit—a result of studying doctrine through scripture—and be prompted to apply the lesson according to our individual needs and not according to group consensus. We would feel inspired instead of inundated.

My husband often accompanies the stake president with whom he serves as counselor as he presides at various meetings. The stake president believes those presiding should speak a word or two to the congregation. He always leans over to my husband during the meeting and asks, "Would you like to say something?" My husband always says, "No," and the president good-naturedly replies, "Do it anyway—and teach them from the scriptures!" I have wondered if I would be prepared to do that on the spur of the moment. Teaching with power from the scriptures is not a gift or responsibility reserved for our Church leaders. How much more confident, powerful, and effective we could be, first in our own lives and then in the lives of others, if we made ourselves more at home in the scriptures! As we drink in the knowledge and power of the inspired word, we will gain the power to discern between truth and falsehood, between the gentle voice of the Spirit, our own compulsive thoughts, and the harassing voices of Satan's imps. Our vision of who we are will sharpen, and our influence will expand. We will be filled with the fruits of the Spirit, which will give us peace and confidence (see Galatians 5:22–23). "Let virtue [the words of Christ] garnish thy thoughts unceasingly; then shall *thy confidence wax strong* in the presence of God; and the doctrine of the priesthood shall distill upon thy soul as the dews from heaven" (D&C 121:45; emphasis added).

2. Come unto Christ and be perfected in him. Many books have been written by members of the Church that help us better understand the Atonement and what it means to be perfected in Christ (see Moroni 10:32). We have learned, with gratitude, that we do not perfect ourselves alone, though some of us have been futilely trying to do so all these years. This is the even better news of the "good news" of the gospel we thought we already understood. These books are a good beginning, but this doctrine will never fully become a part of us and permeate our being until we drink it full strength from the scriptures and teachings of the living prophets. We must never stop seeking to understand it and the other doctrines of the gospel, which are all tied to it. We will never reach our full potential as daughters of God if we ignore or underutilize the scriptures and the doctrine of the Atonement.

Thus, though I have far to go in my study and understanding, I unequivocally bear testimony that all the answers to life's problems are found in the doctrine of the atonement of Jesus Christ, which is the central message of the holy scriptures and the teachings of the living prophets. I can bear this testimony because I know for myself that nothing else works in the end.

A few years ago, I was helping my husband, Brent, with a book on repentance. As I edited his work and read the scriptures and the prophetic teachings he had quoted, I learned that repentance is a lifelong state we must be in, not a place we just visit occasionally when we really mess up and commit big sins. As I began to understand this, the Spirit whispered to me that I was not allowing the atonement of Jesus Christ to operate in my life. I was trying to do it all myself. He wanted to help me, but I wouldn't let him. I thought that the more I did on my own and the less I bothered him, the more faithful I was proving to be.

I made the same mistake about what constitutes faithfulness as the Apostle Peter did before he had the benefit of the Holy Ghost in his life (which came only after the Savior's death). I like Peter a lot. Like me, he often seemed to put his foot in his mouth. He meant well, and his passionate and loving heart was in the right place, but he was often overzealous to show his devotion. He had to learn some things the hard way, like I did. After the Apostles had partaken of the Passover meal at the Last Supper, Jesus "riseth from supper, and laid aside his garments; and took a towel, and girded himself. After that he poureth water into a bason, and began to wash the disciples' feet, and to

wipe them with the towel wherewith he was girded."
Peter, who could hardly fathom the idea that the Son of
God would be washing his dusty, dirty feet—a job usually
relegated to a house servant—protested when the Lord
came to him. "Lord, dost thou wash my feet?" He must
have been incredulous that the others had sat still for it.
Patiently "Jesus answered and said unto him, What I do
thou knowest not now; but thou shalt know hereafter."
Too impetuous to wait for understanding, Peter zealously
exclaimed, "Thou shalt never wash my feet[!]" He thought
he was being faithful by keeping his God from stooping so
low, but Jesus taught him in one sentence the plan of salvation and the essence of what it means to come unto
Christ. The Savior simply said, "If I wash thee not, thou
hast no part with me" (John 13:4–8). If we do not let him
serve us and wash us clean and make us new, no matter
how faithful we think we are being, we have no part with
him. We cannot save or free ourselves. He alone can free
us from Satan's grasp and the effects of the Fall, including
not just sin but absolutely everything that keeps us from
being like him. Other gimmicks may seem to have a temporary effect, but "if the Son therefore shall make you free,
ye shall be free indeed" (John 8:36).

Many members of the Church are familiar with
Stephen E. Robinson's book *Believing Christ*, in which he
so articulately helps us understand the Atonement. My
husband, a colleague of Steve's, heard him share the following thought on the same subject at a daily prayer meeting of the BYU Religious Education faculty. We loved it so

much that, with his permission, we have shared it whenever and wherever we can. It is most hopeful and helpful.

All the negative aspects of human existence brought about by the Fall, Jesus Christ absorbed into himself. He experienced vicariously in Gethsemane all the private griefs and heartaches, all the physical pains and handicaps, all the emotional burdens and depressions of the human family. He knows the loneliness of those who don't fit in, or who aren't handsome or pretty. He knows what it's like to choose up teams and be the last one chosen. He knows the anguish of parents whose children go wrong. He knows these things personally and intimately because he lived them in the Gethsemane experience. Having personally lived a perfect life, he then chose to experience our imperfect lives. In that infinite Gethsemane experience, the meridian of time, the center of eternity, he lived a billion billion lifetimes of sin, pain, disease, and sorrow.

God has no magic wand with which to simply wave bad things into nonexistence. The sins that he remits, he remits by making them his own and suffering them. The pain and heartache that he relieves, he relieves by suffering them himself. These things can be transferred, but they cannot be simply wished or waved away. They must be suffered. Thus we owe him not only for our spiritual cleansing from sin but for our physical, mental, and emotional healings as well, for he has borne these infirmities for us also. All that the Fall put wrong, the Savior in his atonement puts right. It is all part of his infinite sacrifice—of his infinite gift. (Stephen E. Robinson, address at Religious Education Prayer Meeting, 12 February 1992)

Thus I learned that the Atonement covers all of what I like to call the flotsam and jetsam of my life, not just the big shipwrecks. (*Flotsam* and *jetsam* are terms for the debris, foam, and various other yucky things that accumulate on the surface of the ocean, especially as it continually beats against the shore.) The word *atone* means "to cover," and I often ask the Lord at the end of the day not only to forgive me for the wrong things I do and think but to heal or cover up the little bits of mental and emotional junk that accumulate in my life. I trust him to cover not only the sins I commit but the things I didn't do although I should or could have. I have faith that he will cover me so that I don't have to match up to someone else but only to his will for me. That is why, when the flotsam and jetsam of our lives seem ready to overwhelm us, we must learn to immerse ourselves in the therapeutic waters of Christ's sacrifice. There is absolutely nothing in mortality that cannot be overcome or healed through his atonement.

Gleaning again from the examples in the scriptures, I am reminded of Father Lehi's dream, in which he saw that the only people who did not get lost in the oppressive mists of worldly cares and temptation were the ones who literally *clung* to the iron rod that ran along the path to the tree of life. Nephi later learned that the rod of iron represented the word of God (see 1 Nephi 8:19; 11:25). From this interpretation, we can further understand that clinging to the rod of iron represents more than just studying and following the scriptures. Indeed, we can deduce that the rod of iron is Jesus Christ himself. For we learn in "the word" that he is "The Word" (see John 1:1), and the only way to "The Word" is through "the word." In a sense, the two are one and the same. We can't truly "come unto Christ" except by searching the scriptures and *clinging* to him through them. I bear testimony that there is no other way!

3. *Focus on Christ.* The Apostle Peter, walking on the water toward Christ in the midst of a tempestuous storm on the Sea of Galilee, is a graphic example of the power available to those who focus and depend on Christ. Peter had power to stay above the water as long as he kept concentrating on his Savior, who stood waiting to receive him with open arms. As soon as he let his focus be distracted by the terrifying turmoil all around him—"when he saw the wind boisterous,"—he became afraid, lost faith, and began to sink (see Matthew 14:25–30). Likewise, keeping our spiritual eyes riveted on Christ through his word frees us from all the negative aspects of the Fall that hold us back.

President Boyd K. Packer has suggested that we can gain power over unworthy thoughts by filling our minds with worthy ones, such as the words to a hymn (see *Teach Ye Diligently* [Salt Lake City: Deseret Book, 1975], 47). When I start to become overwhelmed, even swallowed up and sucked down, by thoughts of my own inadequacy and unworthiness, I have learned to fill my mind with thoughts of Christ. I get out my scriptures and read until I am filled with the power of his Spirit. I also love to play a Mormon Tabernacle Choir CD I have nearly worn out, entitled *O Divine Redeemer* (Salt Lake City: Bonneville Classics, 1992). All the songs are about Christ, including my favorite, "When I Survey the Wondrous Cross." I am so profoundly moved by this song. Even though it speaks of the kind of pride in superiority that we all must battle, it always humbles me and makes me realize how petty, wasteful, and prideful is my selfish obsession with my own *inferiority*. How can I obsess so much about myself when I fully realize what Christ has suffered for me?

When I survey the wondrous cross
On which the Prince of glory died,
My richest gain I count but loss
And pour contempt on all my pride.

Forbid it, Lord, that I should boast,
Save in the death of Christ, my God!
All the vain things that charm me most,
I sacrifice them to his blood.

See from his head, his hands, his feet,
Sorrow and love flow mingled down.
Did e'er such love and sorrow meet,
Or thorns compose so rich a crown?

Were the whole realm of nature mine,
That were a present far too small;
Love so amazing, so divine,
Demands my soul, my life, my all!

—Isaac Watts

Temple worship is another way of focusing on Christ, especially as we listen carefully to the words of instruction there rather than dwell on our distractions. Fasting and serving out of true charity also help us direct our focus to him. When turmoil and fear all around threaten to confuse and confound us, we must put on blinders like the horses on a racetrack who must concentrate only on reaching the finish line. It is ironic that when we actually tune out our problems, inadequacies, and "the wind boisterous," and focus on Christ only, we come to see everything more clearly and in its proper perspective. He is the one and only thing we can always depend on—the one true compass, the only sure foundation.

4. *Seek and share the pure love of Christ.* When we feel inadequate and unloved, it may be a sign that we are thinking too much about ourselves. This is a good time to forget about ourselves and to love and serve others with charity, the pure love of Christ. Any of us, no matter how untalented, inadequate, or nontraditional we may feel, can and *must* develop the gift of charity. After the Apostle Paul taught the Corinthians about the diversity of spiritual gifts and talents among the members of the Church, he then declared, "And yet shew I unto you a more excellent way" (1 Corinthians 12:31)—something even more important than all of them. He went on to give the majestic discourse on charity cited previously (see 1 Corinthians 13). Like a magic, healing balm that regenerates all who touch it, charity embraces, warms, and uplifts both the giver and the receiver. This salient eternal truth is set forth in a simple Primary song:

Jesus said love ev'ryone;
Treat them kindly, too.
When your heart is filled with love,
Others will love you.

("Jesus Said Love Everyone," Children's Songbook
[Salt Lake City: The Church of Jesus Christ of Latter-
day Saints, 1989], 61)

Not only will others love us, but we will feel Christ's love for us. Nothing, not even perfect self-love, could make us feel better about ourselves.

5. *Discover and do the will of Christ.* "Come unto me, all ye that labour and are heavy laden, and I will give you rest. Take my yoke upon you, and learn of me; for I am meek and lowly in heart: and ye shall find rest unto your souls. For my yoke is easy, and my burden is light" (Matthew 11:28–30). This basically sums up the entire matter. Coming unto Christ and letting him do for us what we cannot do for ourselves is the answer to every problem we face. He will never set an impossible standard for us or expect us to exhaust ourselves in that which is of no worth. He will never ask more than we can give, for his yoke is easier and his burden is lighter than any other burden we can take upon ourselves. All he asks in return for relieving us of our burdens is that we seek and do his will, which always brings us peace—spiritual rest—not the insanity we sometimes bring on ourselves. As we simply live his gospel, trust in him, and do his will to the best of our understanding and ability, he will, in his own time, take care of those things over which we have no power.

Being in harmony with the Lord's will for us individually is the greatest state we can attain in life. The following poem, attributed to Henry Wadsworth Longfellow, has been a guiding influence for me ever since I first found it as a teenager. However, after all these years, I am still working at achieving this "inward stillness."

> *Let us then labor for an inward stillness,*
> *An inward stillness and an inward healing,*
> *That perfect silence where lips and heart*
> *Are still, and we no longer entertain*
> *Our own imperfect thought and vain opinions,*
> *But God alone speaks in us, and we wait*
> *In singleness of heart, that we may know*
> *His will, and in the silence of our spirits,*
> *We may do his will and do that only!*

(A Collection of Inspirational Verse for Latter-day Saints, comp. Bryan B. Gardner and Calvin T. Broadhead [Salt Lake City: Bookcraft, 1963], 81)

Daughters of Christ

When we come unto Christ through faithfully immersing ourselves in the scriptures, partaking of the doctrine of his atonement, continually focusing and refocusing on him, sharing his love with others, and seeking to know and do his will, we automatically tap into the powers of God. We become new and doubly powerful creatures, now being not only daughters of our Heavenly Father but also spiritually begotten daughters of Christ. As King Benjamin explained to his beloved people who had committed themselves to the gospel, "And now, because of the covenant which ye have made ye shall be called the children of Christ, his sons, and his daughters; for behold, this day he hath spiritually begotten you; for ye say that your hearts are changed through faith on his name; therefore, ye are born of him and have become his sons and his daughters" (Mosiah 5:7).

Great endowments and capacities come to the daughters of Christ. Speaking at the 1981 general women's meeting, President Ezra Taft Benson endorsed these words written to him by one Relief Society sister:

> The great strength of a good woman—a saint, if you will—is her personal testimony of the Savior and her faith in his spokesmen, the prophet and the Apostles of Jesus Christ. If she follows them, she will have the countenance of Christ for her beauty, the peace of Christ to support her emotionally, the Savior's example as a means to solve her problems and to strengthen her, and the love of Christ as the source of love for herself, her family, and those about her. She can be sure of herself . . . and find joy and fulfillment in her role. ("The Honored Place of Woman," *Ensign*, November 1981, 107)

As a daughter of Christ, I have had enough experience with him to comprehend that he does not need to be a woman to understand how women feel, for "he cometh into the world that he may save all men if they will hearken unto his voice; for behold, he suffereth the pains of all men, yea, the pains of every living creature, both men, *women*, and children, who belong to the family of Adam" (2 Nephi 9:21; emphasis added). I can tell by the way he nurtures me and the way my prayers are answered that he understands me completely—even better than I understand myself. Because he understands me, and each of us, so perfectly, he has the power to free us. No thing and no one else has the power to do this for us, nor can we do it for ourselves. It is indeed as King Benjamin confidently declared: "Under this head ye are made free, and there is *no other head* whereby ye can be made free" (Mosiah 5:8; emphasis added).

3
Free from the Priesthood Question

There are issues concerning our relationships to and with men that can keep us from finding complete freedom as women. One day a young husband, troubled about his wife's struggle with some of these issues, walked into my husband's office in the Joseph Smith Building at BYU. Desperate for some answers, he had been referred to Brother Top, and he had come to ask my husband for help in reaching his disconcerted wife as she wrestled with the "priesthood question." It seemed she was even drifting away from the Church because she couldn't find answers that satisfied her. My husband talked with the young man for a while and tried to reassure him. However, he worried that the information he was giving the distraught husband to pass on to his wife might ring a little hollow coming from a man. Therefore, knowing my interest in the subject, he suggested that the young man bring his wife to meet with me. In preparation for the meeting, I had to organize my thoughts. The young woman never came to meet me, but if she had, this is what I would have told her:

Why don't women hold the priesthood? The definitive answer to this question is: We don't know. The Lord has not yet seen fit to reveal the exact reasons for the way he has divided responsibilities between men and women. President Gordon B. Hinckley once declared that "only the Lord, through revelation, could alter that situation. He has not done so, so it is profitless for us to speculate and worry about it" ("Ten Gifts from the Lord," *Ensign,* November 1985, 86).

However, we must again acknowledge that perhaps the real, deeper question women are asking is this: "Am I truly a man's equal in the sight of God?" I believe this is a fair and vital question, and we *do* know some things that can provide us with at least a limited understanding on this issue. The following represents some of what I have searched out over the years. The greater principle I have gleaned, not only from research but even more from actual experience, is that women have no *need* to hold and exercise priesthood because they have powers and influence of their own.

Different but Equal from the Beginning

Let's begin at the beginning, with Eve, keeping in mind that the First Presidency of the Church declared that "gender is an essential characteristic of individual premortal, mortal, and eternal identity and purpose" ("The Family: A Proclamation to the World," *Ensign,* November

1995, 102). We do not need to turn women into men to make them valuable. Women have had their own remarkable set of God-given characteristics since the time of Eve. These qualities are meant to be complementary to and fully equal to those bestowed upon Adam and the rest of the male race. "It is not good for man to be alone," President Ezra Taft Benson affirmed, "because a righteous woman complements what may be lacking in man's natural personality and disposition. Paul said: 'Neither is the man without the woman, neither the woman without the man, in the Lord' (1 Corinthians 11:11). Nowhere is this complementary association more ideally portrayed than in the eternal marriage of our first parents—Adam and Eve" (*Teachings of Ezra Taft Benson* [Salt Lake City: Bookcraft, 1988], 547).

In an address to the eleventh annual conference of Collegium Aesculapium on the role of Eve, Beverly Campbell, then director of International Affairs for the LDS Church, commented on the passage in Genesis in which Eve is called a "help meet" for Adam:

> Society would have us believe that a help meet is a person of lesser stature—a subject, a subordinate.
>
> An examination of the word itself yields an altogether different meaning. The *Oxford English Dictionary* lists its meaning as "even with or equal to." The original Hebrew text is even more enlightening. The word that has been translated as

"help meet" is a combination of two root words: *ezer* and *k'enegdo.*

The word *ezer* also combines two roots: the first meaning "to rescue" or "to save" or "as a savior," sometimes coupled with the concept of majesty, and the other meaning "strength" or "to be strong."

The second Hebrew word, *k'enegdo,* is identified as meaning "equal."

Suppose we all, male and female alike, had been raised to read Genesis 2:18 as follows: "It is not good that man should be alone: I will make a majestic, saving power, equal with him, to be his companion." Surely attitudes, laws, and customs would be different, and the relationships that God intended would more naturally and more easily exist. (*Mother Eve: Mentor for Today's Woman: A Heritage of Honor,* address given 2 April 1993, Salt Lake City, Utah)

Unfortunately, misunderstanding of this term *help meet* and the proper role of woman that it describes has been the source of much suffering and oppression of women through the centuries. Perhaps further misunderstanding of the equality of the woman's role stems from the passage in Genesis in which Eve is told of the conditions that will be *placed upon her in mortality.* She is informed, "In sorrow thou shalt bring forth children; and thy desire shall be to thy husband, and he shall rule over thee" (Genesis 3:16). Like the "curses" of hard work that were put upon Adam *for his sake* (see v. 17), we assume that these "curses" or conditions put upon Eve were also *for her sake*. We are willing to admit that work and sweat and toil are, in truth, blessings to all human beings. Many will even admit that the pain and travail of childbearing is a sanctifying pain that helps create the unsurpassed bond between mother and child. Surely, then, there is blessing and divine purpose behind the Lord's injunction that a husband should "rule" over his wife.

President Spencer W. Kimball prophetically suggested that the word *preside* more accurately depicts the patriarchal role than does *rule* (see "The Blessings and Responsibilities of Womanhood," *Ensign*, March 1976, 72). This changes the role from one of dominance to one of service. Dr. Robert L. Millet, dean of Religious Education at Brigham Young University, offers the insight that although there are "presiding officers in all divinely appointed organizations, including the family," the marriage relationship is a partnership and not a hierarchy like the Church organization.

> The family or patriarchal order is a partnership, with father and mother counseling together, in conjunction with the children, toward the resolution of family challenges and difficulties. The Church and the home are both divine institutions, and their modes of government are inspired. But attempting to apply one system of government to the other institution may lead to serious problems. For example, the family is not hierarchical in

nature, even though it is presided over by the father. The Church is not a partnership, although people in the ward must work together in love and harmony. ("Restoring the Patriarchal Order," address given 31 July 1996, Genealogy and Family History Conference of Brigham Young University, Provo, Utah, typescript in possession of author, 15–17)

Thus, the patriarchal order in the home could perhaps be considered "order among equals."

The prophets have often spoken of the innate spirituality of women. In 1913, Elder Francis M. Lyman of the Quorum of the Twelve taught that the priesthood brethren "should be the leaders, but in some instances wives are stronger in the faith, stronger in spirituality and in the gifts and graces of the Lord than men, and much is required of them" (in Conference Report, October 1913, 37). More recently, Elder Dallin H. Oaks explained that he was "persuaded that women are generally more spiritual than men. Perhaps this is because their unique gift of child-bearing, which places them at the wellspring of life, makes them more sensitive to eternal verities" (*Pure in Heart* [Salt Lake City: Bookcraft, 1988], 123).

Is it possible that Eve's spiritual understanding and desires to progress in righteousness were slightly stronger and more urgent than Adam's? Could this be why Eve partook of the forbidden fruit before Adam? Undoubtedly, she knew—however limited that knowledge may have been—that something had to take place in order for them to obtain mortal bodies, to multiply and replenish the earth, and eventually to become like their heavenly parents. She meant well by initiating the process. However, she made the decision on her own, without consulting with Adam first. They had been commanded to be one flesh (see Genesis 2:24), but she had made a major decision without him, one that left him no other righteous choice but to follow after her. Could this be the reason that, *as a condition of mortality,* Eve and her daughters were placed behind their husbands in this regard, instead of beside them? Eliza R. Snow, a very independent woman but an ardent defender of the presiding authority of priesthood, seemed to imply such an idea in her poetry.

> *Woman*
> *. . . led in the transgression, and was plac'd*
> *By Eloheim's unchangeable decree,*
> *In a subservient and dependent sphere*

According to Jill C. Mulvay, who quoted the above poem in an article for *BYU Studies:* "Countless times in her travels, Sister Snow enlarged upon that doctrine for her sisters. In the beginning, she explained, male and female were addressed as one, but the Fall brought about a change, and thus the 'curse of Eve' rested upon all womankind" ("Eliza R. Snow and the Woman Question," *BYU Studies,* vol. 16, no. 2 (1976), 259).

Perhaps we need to learn that we must never get out ahead of our husbands and leave them behind, spiritually speaking. They cannot achieve exaltation without us, and neither can we make it without them. Decisions must be made and actions must be taken in unison.

Essential Differences

A husband's role in presiding over his wife does not consist of telling her what to do but of taking the responsibility to see that decisions made by both of them together are implemented. What better way to strengthen a man's spiritual nature than by giving him the responsibility of priesthood leadership? The Lord often sends us to earth in situations that require us to develop the very strengths we lack. What more perfect system could there be for men and women than the Lord's inspired plan? Women learn to cooperate with and benefit from the more physical nature of men, while men learn to trust in and be blessed and directed by the more spiritual nature of women. Yet somehow they work together as full equals and become one with each other and with God. Elder John A. Widtsoe elaborated on these God-given traits of men and women:

> This recognition of natural function appears in the organization of the Church. By divine fiat, the Priesthood is conferred on the men. This means that organization must prevail in the family, the ultimate unit of the Church. The husband, the Priesthood bearer, presides over the family; the Priesthood conferred upon him is intended for the blessing of the whole family. Every member shares in the gift bestowed, but under a proper

organization. No man who understands the gospel believes that he is greater than his wife, or more beloved of the Lord, because he holds the Priesthood, but rather that he is under the responsibility of speaking and acting for the family in official matters. It is a protection to the woman who, because of her motherhood, is under a large physical and spiritual obligation. *Motherhood is an eternal part of Priesthood.* It is a wise provision that the man, who is the freer to move about both at home and abroad, should be called to the family presidency and be under the responsibility of holding the Priesthood. This does not limit equality among men and women. Citizens in a free land are not unequal because some hold office and others do not (*Evidences and Reconciliations,* arranged by G. Homer Durham [Salt Lake City: Bookcraft, 1960], 307–8; emphasis added).

What will happen to civilization if women desert their own gifts in a blind stampede to assume the more physical nature of men, which they may think is more desirable or effective? The predominantly physical nature of men and the primarily spiritual nature of women are both needed to keep civilization and the plan of salvation in balance. Other civilizations have traditionally (though perhaps not always in practice) recognized the importance of this congenial, complementary relationship.

My husband and I once had occasion to visit two different Japanese gardens, one in Oregon and the other in

California. At the entrance to each stood two fierce and formidable-looking "lion dogs"—a cross between a lion and a dog—one on each side of the gateway. In appearance, size, and prominence, they were exactly alike. However, our guides explained to us that one was male and the other female. How could we tell the difference? The male lion dog stood with one paw on top of a globe, representing the world and symbolizing his responsibility over the physical life. On the other hand, the female stood with her paw over a lion dog cub, representing her stewardship over the spiritual life. Stable, righteous family and social life on earth and resurrected, eternal family life are a perfected combination of both the physical and the spiritual.

Finally, Elder James E. Talmage indicated that "the curse of Eve" may be a condition placed on her only in mortality, and that she may one day fully be one in the priesthood with her husband:

> In the restored Church of Jesus Christ, the Holy Priesthood is conferred, as an individual bestowal, upon men only, and this in accordance with Divine requirement. It is not given to woman to exercise the authority of the Priesthood *independently*; nevertheless, in the sacred endowments associated with the ordinances pertaining to the House of the Lord, woman shares with man the blessings of the priesthood. When the frailties and imperfections of mortality are left behind, in the glorified state of the blessed hereafter, husband and wife will

administer in their respective stations, seeing and understanding alike, and co-operating to the full in the government of their family kingdom. Then shall woman be recompensed in rich measure for all the injustice that womanhood has endured in mortality. Then shall woman reign by Divine right, a queen in the resplendent realm of her glorified state, even as exalted man shall stand, priest and king unto the Most High God. Mortal eye cannot see nor mind comprehend the beauty, glory, and majesty of a righteous woman made perfect in the celestial kingdom of God. (James E. Talmage, "The Eternity of Sex," *Young Woman's Journal* 25 (October 1914): 602–3; emphasis added)

Less Visible Does Not Mean Less Valuable

Most of us have heard the above reasoning about women and the priesthood before, but there is another sobering aspect of this situation that is not always mentioned or acknowledged. I learned this from a friend named FloBeth Keller. FloBeth was quite familiar with other churches and their concepts of women and priesthood. She was studying to become a Methodist minister herself when she met her future husband, Roger Keller, a Presbyterian minister. She was comfortable with the idea of complementary roles within a marriage and family, so she gave up her own career and stayed at home to raise their children. While researching a book in defense of the

LDS Church (under attack by the anti-Mormon group that produced the film *The Godmakers*), her husband was converted to the restored gospel and baptized. As FloBeth subsequently investigated the Church herself and discovered that Latter-day Saint women were not ordained to the priesthood, she struggled to understand a woman's relationship to God and her role within the Church as taught in Latter-day Saint theology. Even though she understood the concept of differing roles, she was troubled to think that perhaps a woman was unable to have the priesthood because her stature in the eyes of God was somehow less than that of a man. Moreover, she wondered if this would somehow limit a woman's opportunities for service in the Church.

Aware of her struggle, an inspired stake president did an unusual thing. He invited her to attend a stake meeting of ward bishoprics. While there surrounded by the sustaining influence of the priesthood, she felt an assurance fill her heart that this division of duties was indeed according to God's plan. She came to understand that women would be fully capable and worthy to hold the priesthood *if God had chosen to divide up the responsibilities in that manner.* This moving experience erased her doubts about the Church, and she also became a member. She found that not having priesthood did not limit her service in the Church at all. Later, while serving as a Relief Society president, she felt that she was able to do as much as she had hoped to do as a Methodist minister and more.

As time went on and FloBeth accepted this divine division of roles, she came to an insightful and profound conclusion about womanhood that has been very influential in my life and in the writing of this book. She observed that although a woman's role is equal in importance and stature with a priesthood holder's, it is not equal in visibility. She learned that a woman's role is very much like that of the Savior—one of sacrifice, of foregoing the honors of this world to accomplish a greater good (see John 5:41). Though men may have a unique understanding of Jesus Christ through priesthood service, women comprehend him through sacrifice in at least two ways: (1) in childbirth, and (2) through often unheralded but deeply influential service.

A mother, like her Savior Jesus Christ, knows the agony and the ecstasy of sacrificing her own body to bring forth life. The pain that bears down relentlessly upon a mother as she brings forth life is, in a small measure, symbolic of the infinite weight of the Atonement that bore down unremittingly upon our Lord in Gethsemane as he brought forth eternal life. Further, the birth of a precious and pure new baby is a type and shadow of the justified and sanctified "new creature" who is born again in Christ (see 2 Corinthians 5:17).

Giving birth is only the beginning of a mother's life of sacrifice. The words *mother* and *sacrifice* could almost be used synonymously. However, women sacrifice in other ways as well. Elder Richard G. Scott of the Quorum of the Twelve pointed out the vulnerable position in which women are placed in society. "I humbly thank our Father in Heaven for His daughters, you who were willing to come to earth to live under such uncertain circumstances," he declared, adding that most men could not live with such uncertainties. He explained:

> Social customs require that you wait to be asked for marriage. You are expected to go with your husband wherever his employment or call takes him. Your environment and neighborhood are determined by his ability to provide, meager or not. You place your life in the Lord's hands each time you bear a child. He makes no such sacrifice. The blessing of nurturing children and caring for a husband is often intermingled with many routine tasks. But you do all these things willingly because you are a woman. Generally you have no idea of how truly wonderful and capable you are, how very much appreciated and loved, or how desperately needed, for most men don't tell you as completely and as often as needed. ("The Joy of Living the Great Plan of Happiness," *Ensign,* November 1996, 75)

This plain and simple truth about a woman's sacrificial role applies just as well to those who are not wives and mothers. Any woman who serves in her family (no matter what its configuration), in the Church, or in the world outside the Church will likely have to face this reality of being less visible. A woman unwilling to accept such a calling in life may never be completely happy in her role or fully realize its potential, just as Christ would have failed in his mission had he selfishly rejected his fore-ordained role and sought for temporal power or fame. On the other hand, a woman with the faith and courage to give up the privileges of station and celebrity in mortality, if necessary, will surely have profound influence in this life and honor, power, and glory in the next. Indeed, as mentioned above, because of sacred promises given to faithful women through the temple ordinances of the gospel of Jesus Christ, we have reason to believe that women may share priesthood authority and power with their husbands in the exalted realms.

Nevertheless, if what we now know of our Mother in Heaven is any indication, women will continue to fill the less visible role in the partnership. Though we understand less of the part our Mother in Heaven plays, her influence is surely as real and necessary as that of our Father in Heaven, though we don't fully comprehend it in mortality. Undoubtedly, she is contented with the lower visibility of her role because she understands the higher capacity of it. Indeed, President Spencer W. Kimball praised the restrained but powerful influence of women here and hereafter. "When we sing that doctrinal hymn and anthem of affection, 'O My Father,' we get a sense of the ultimate in maternal modesty, of the restrained, queenly elegance of our Heavenly Mother, and knowing how profoundly our mortal mothers have shaped us here, do we suppose her influence on us as individuals to be less if we live so as to return there?" (in Conference Report, April 1978, 7).

This is not to say that a woman never gets recognition or position in this life, or that a man never works humbly behind the scenes. In more ways than not, the roles of men and women are very much the same. Service knows no gender except in the limited areas of priesthood responsibility and childbearing.

Women Don't Need to Hold the Priesthood

A woman who understands and has tasted of the profound and expansive power and influence of righteous womanhood has no need and feels no desire to hold the priesthood. However, in order to experience and fully develop her own power, she must be willing to forego the honors and attention of the world, the craving for control over others, and the gratification of immediate results. (A man who wanted to exercise priesthood power would have to do likewise.) As in the popular song "The Wind beneath My Wings"—which tells of one who can fly higher than an eagle because of the quiet, unseen support of a loved one—a woman must be willing to work patiently and sometimes invisibly.

In addition, a woman must always keep in mind that though the eagle is more visible and commands immediate attention and admiration, the wind is, in some ways, more powerful and its influence more far reaching and long lasting. A woman's influence can be equal to and in some cases even exceed the influence of a man—but only if she is careful not to lose the remarkable substance of power she has in her hand while grasping at the shadow of the priesthood, which she does not have *independently* in mortality. With this object in view, I would like to share some of the ways in which I have discovered my own equality of worth and mission and the remarkable power I have. In the next two chapters, I will suggest some practical ways in which women can exercise such power and influence both at home and in the Church as an equal complement to the priesthood power of men.

The Sacred Male-Female Relationship in the Home

Those of us who are grateful for the feminine characteristics and womanly strengths we have been given desire
to promote the virtues of linking womanhood and manhood together in a fully equal partnership. We want
women to be treated as equally valuable because our char-
acter traits complement men's, not because they compete
with them. We would like the differences between men
and women to be not only accepted but celebrated, uti-
lized, and accentuated for the betterment of all. Nowhere
is this more important than in the family.

Though many in the world think it tyranny that a man
should be the "head" of the family, righteous priesthood
holders have always recognized their true "servant-leader"
role and the sacred and respected role of women. Consider
how Adam revered his companion, Eve, "the mother of all
living" (see Moses 4:26). Recall that Abraham was commanded by the Lord to "hearken unto [Sarah's] voice"
(Genesis 21:12). In our age, President Howard W. Hunter

admonished the brethren of the priesthood, as had many before him, to have reverence for motherhood and, implicitly, for womanhood: "The First Presidency has said: 'Motherhood is near to divinity. It is the highest, holiest service to be assumed by mankind.' The priesthood cannot work out its destiny, nor can God's purposes be fulfilled, without our helpmates. *Mothers perform a labor the priesthood cannot do.* For this gift of life, the priesthood should have love unbounded for the mothers of their children" ("Being a Righteous Husband and Father," *Ensign,* November 1994, 50; emphasis added).

Holding the uniquely sacred and exalted calling of motherhood along with the specialized gifts that accompany it, and having absolutely no blessing of the priesthood withheld from us other than the administrative exercising of it, how can women expect to have the priesthood also? Perhaps we have fallen into Satan's trap and do not believe or perceive the holy privilege and power that is ours. Worse yet, perhaps we are not content with the God-given mission bestowed upon us and want to alter and distort it to suit our own selfish ends. Where would it leave our husbands, sons and brothers if we held the priesthood also? How needed would they be? What unique calling would belong to them?

This idea that it is our very differences that make men and women both feel vital and needed in the family structure came home to me in a very practical way once. I was up in the middle of the night with a sick child who, like most children, wanted mother when she was sick. Being very tired, I envied my husband who slept on undisturbed by our daughter's crying. I didn't really expect him to get up; he had to work the next day and would not be able to take a nap as I could at home. However, Janey, my agitated daughter, about four years old at the time, impatiently insisted that I go and get Dad. Puzzled and feeling a bit rejected, I asked, "Why do you want Dad?" Annoyed that I was so "clueless," Janey irascibly blurted out, "To give me a blessing, what do you think?!" I was delighted to awaken my husband and have him share some of the responsibility for the care of our sick daughter. I was really thankful that I couldn't do it all myself. Why would any woman want the priesthood on top of all the other responsibilities placed upon her?

Some women would answer that question: "Because that is the only way that women will ever overcome oppression and be equal to men!" Admittedly, some women have found themselves in marriages or other situations in which men have exercised unrighteous dominion in the name of priesthood. But when the priesthood is exercised righteously, as the Lord intended when he set up the relationship between Adam and Eve, a woman will never feel oppressed or subservient or unequal to her husband. She will feel that she is the queen of her home. In the talk cited earlier, President Hunter went on to add:

> A man who holds the priesthood accepts his wife as a partner in the leadership of the home and family with full knowledge of and full participation in all decisions relating thereto. Of necessity there must be in the Church and in the home a

presiding officer (see D&C 107:21). By divine appointment, the responsibility to preside in the home rests upon the priesthood holder (see Moses 4:22). . . . Presiding in righteousness necessitates a shared responsibility between husband and wife: together you act with knowledge and participation in all family matters. For a man to operate independent of or without regard to the feelings and counsel of his wife in governing the family is to exercise unrighteous dominion. ("Being a Righteous Husband and Father," 50–51)

Though my husband presides in our home, in actual practice we are so united that we function as one. He is also *my* "help meet." Sometimes he is inspired; sometimes I get the revelation. Sometimes I have the better idea; at other times he makes more sense. His strengths often pick up where my weaknesses leave off, and vice versa. In some instances I correct him, and sometimes he has to set me back on course. The two of us together, with all our differences, fare better than we would if we were exactly alike or if one of us were missing.

Let me give an everyday illustration of how this works in my life. Very seldom does my husband speak up and advise me not to do something that I have planned. Yet without exception, when he has told me that he doesn't feel right about something and I have gone ahead and done it anyway (he never forbids me), I have been painfully sorry.

For example, one summer we took our family to

California to vacation while my husband, Brent, presented several *Know Your Religion* lectures there. We had been in California for several days, and I had not yet seen the ocean or shown my children their first beach. Brent was not as thrilled about the beach as I was, and I began to doubt that he would ever take us to see it. So one evening when he was scheduled to lecture, I decided to take matters into my own hands. I announced that we would be taking the car to search for the ocean while he was speaking. A dubious look came over his face as he knitted his eyebrows in concern. He didn't try to forbid me, but ventured, "I don't think that's a good idea. Why don't you wait?" Doubting that waiting on him would ever get me to the beach, I told him we would be fine. We were within a few miles of the coast; I figured that every coastal town had a beach, and if I just drove west I would inevitably find it.

In spite of the warning flag that went up in my mind because of past experiences with disregarding Brent's counsel, I loaded my children into our huge, boxy, brown station wagon and set out for the Pacific Ocean. I now also had another purpose in my mind. I had to show my husband that I wasn't completely dependent on him and could do things on my own.

The one thing I had banked on was the idea that most of California had sunny, flat beaches like those in southern California. However, we were in the central part of the state, and I soon began to discover that not all California beaches are alike. Or are they? I still don't know because I literally became "lost in a fog." The road I had followed out of town—which, according to my reading of the map, should have led to the beach—became narrower and less traveled as we went west. Pretty soon we found ourselves on a gravel road through what seemed to be some kind of private, fenced land. I saw a sign about a state park, but I couldn't tell exactly where it was pointing. There was only one way to go anyway. At this point the road became one little dirt lane. There was not another car in sight, and the fog got denser and denser until I could see only a few feet in front of the car. Instead of descending down to a beach as I thought it should, the trail rose higher and higher. It got really spooky. It was like a highway into the "Twilight Zone." I finally had to swallow my pride and try to turn the "big brown bomber" station wagon around before I sacrificed my children driving off the edge of some cliff.

The whole thing was a wasted, frustrating effort, and I dreaded having my husband ask how we had fared. Yet I knew it wasn't because I was incompetent or incapable that my plans had been thwarted, but because I had disregarded inspired counsel from the man who officially represents the Lord in my home. I had ignored the Lord's commandment to be united in decision making.

On the other hand, patriarchs are better leaders when they in turn recognize and heed a woman's inspired counsel. I believe that a woman's greatest contribution to any relationship is her heightened sensitivity not only to spiritual things but to emotional needs and problems as well. I like to compare this aspect of a woman's role at home, in the Church, and in the world to the nerve endings in the body, which sense the needs and feelings of the body and report them to the brain through the spinal cord, the brain being the Godhead and the spinal cord being the priesthood or backbone of the body. It is a perfect and remarkable system, yet without each one of its components, the body is lame.

I am more "in touch" than my husband is with such emotional things. For instance, I am usually the one to sense when there is something amiss with my children. I will study and pray about the problem and then talk to Brent about it, suggesting a father's interview or blessing or a family home evening that might be helpful. When I see that Brent is getting too busy to remember family prayer and scripture reading, I am usually the one who gets us going again, though I have had to learn to do it without taking over or nagging. Sometimes I have to "set things up" so that he will remember to perform his priesthood/patriarchal duties.

Robert Millet suggests that this was the situation in marriages anciently as well. He cites the pattern of Rebekah and Isaac as one example of the shared responsibility in the marriage partnership, referring to the instance in which an inspired Rebekah arranged without her husband's knowledge for Jacob, the worthy son, to receive the birthright blessing from Isaac instead of the unrighteous Esau, who had sold his birthright and married outside the covenant. Millet concludes:

> If we might be so bold, we might suggest that on this occasion Isaac was not as much in tune with the workings of the Spirit and the mind of

God as was Rebekah, and that it took her inspired intervention to bring about the purposes of the Lord. This admission in no way minimizes the greatness and importance of Isaac, one who . . . has ascended the throne of godhood [D&C 132:37]. It does point up, nonetheless, that the patriarchal order is a family order, a partnership, a joint stewardship. [Quoting Elder Bruce R. McConkie:] "It is an eternal principle—the man and the woman are not alone: neither is the man without the woman, nor the woman without the man in the Lord. Women are appointed, Rebekah-like, to be guides and lights in righteousness in the family unit, and to engineer and arrange so that things are done in the way that will result in the salvation of more of our Father's children" (McConkie, *Ensign*, January 1979, 63). ("Restoring the Patriarchal Order," address given 31 July 1996, Genealogy and Family History Conference of Brigham Young University, Provo, Utah, typescript in possession of author, 8–9)

Most of the time, however, it is uncanny how much my husband and I think and act in spontaneous unity, as if we share the same mind and heart. It gives me a glimpse of what it means to be "one, even as . . . [God the Father and Jesus Christ] are one" (John 17:22). Indeed, the Apostle Paul explains that the man is the head of the woman, Christ is the head of the man, and God the Father is the head of Christ. Yet we learn throughout scripture that the Father and the Son are "one God, yea, the very Eternal Father of heaven and of earth" (Mosiah 15:4), and we are to be "one" with them (see 1 Corinthians 11:3; John 17:21). No wonder marriage in the patriarchal order is required for godhood!

However, a woman need not be a wife to do her part in support of the Lord's priesthood program. Daughters, sisters, and other women living in a family relationship with priesthood holders can also play important complementary roles. This principle was dramatically illustrated to Dorothea Speth Condie, wife of Spencer J. Condie of the First Quorum of the Seventy, when she was a child in Dresden, Germany, during World War II. One night her house was firebombed, and the family attempted to escape the fire raging through the streets by making their way to the Elbe River.

> For safety, we did not all walk together. My father took one of my older sisters and my twin sister and began to lead the way. My mother, my oldest sister, and I were to follow as closely as possible. As my father started walking, he headed towards a narrow side street instead of choosing the wide street which led directly to our goal, to the river. Mother stopped, not wanting to follow down the narrow, burning street and began calling Dad to try to persuade him to turn around and take the more direct route along our street, which seemed so much safer and quicker. But due to the

firestorm, Dad could not hear her plea, and he continued walking along the narrow side street.

With each passing second, the distance between us increased, but Mom was still not willing to abandon her plan. Then I heard my older sister plead with her, "Mom, let's follow Dad; he holds the Priesthood!" With this reminder, we started to move quickly, trying to catch up with Dad, who led us safely in a roundabout way down to the river.

The family later learned from a neighbor that she and her husband had taken the very street that Dorothea's father had avoided. The neighbor's husband, who was ahead of her leading the way had stepped onto the street only to be engulfed before her eyes in tentacles of fiery flames. The street had been covered with liquid phosphorus from a bomb. This chemical was invisible, but immediately ignited when stepped on. The woman could do nothing for her unfortunate husband. She was lucky to save herself by turning around and choosing another way (Dorothea Speth Condie, "Let's Follow Dad—He Holds the Priesthood," in *Behind the Iron Curtain: Recollections of Latter-day Saints in East Germany, 1945–1989*, coll. and trans. Garold N. Davis and Norma S. Davis [Provo: BYU Studies, 1996], 33–34).

One sister played an important role in supporting her younger brother as he struggled to remain a worthy priesthood holder. She had left home shortly after he was born, and they had not gotten to know each other well.

However, when he moved with his parents to a new community and began to become inactive in the Church, his sister became concerned enough to reach out to him. She often sent letters or made phone calls expressing her love for him and pleading with him to stay close to his family and the Church. She and his parents persisted until he repented and returned to full activity.

Her efforts came back to bless her years later, when that brother administered a priesthood blessing to her and her children one evening after her husband had abandoned them and taken their family savings. At that time, he seemed to see in her eyes the question, "Why were you able to honor the priesthood and my husband was not?" As he reflected on the answer to that question, he realized that she had been one of the major influences in his life and had "played a significant role in why [he] was worthy to bless her and her children that evening" (Rhett G. Wintch, "A Blessing for My Sister," *Ensign*, March 1996, 66). These are just a couple of examples of the righteous influence women of all ages can have on priesthood holders and men in general in the family.

The "different but equal" status we enjoy as LDS women can offer us and the women of the world the dignity and respect we deserve without our sacrificing all that we hold dear in family life. Where else is a woman so thoroughly and even doctrinally encouraged to be a queen in her home and an educated, prepared, self-sufficient, contributing member of society as well? Where else is a woman promised that she may be a queen, a priestess, and even a goddess throughout eternity if she is "merely" a righteous woman and, at some point, a worthy wife and mother? Where else are men considered as only "first among equals" and repeatedly urged to preside with love rather than rule with fear in their families? These are only some of the objectives we seek to share with our sisters through the gospel of Jesus Christ. It is God's perfect system and the only way to true, enduring joy for both women and men.

Men and Women in the Church

The complementary characteristics of men and women that bless the home work within the institutional Church as well. Perhaps women don't realize the profound influence they have on the Church even though they do not sit in its governing priesthood councils. Their innate desires to serve and uplift others draw them naturally to church service, while priesthood responsibilities and privileges beckon to men who, in general, might otherwise be less inclined toward religion. FloBeth Keller, the convert mentioned previously who wrestled with the fact that LDS women could not be ordained to the priesthood, observed that in other churches where there is no lay priesthood, men tend to be less active than women.

The sincere service of a woman is as acceptable and blessed by God as that of a priesthood holder, whether the world knows anything about it or not. In fact, the teachings of Christ in the New Testament seem to indicate that people are even more blessed when they serve secretly or quietly. Those who serve to be seen by others receive the fleeting satisfaction of fickle mortal praise, while those who do not seek such public applause receive the greater reward of an all-powerful and eternal God. "How can ye believe," asked the Savior, "which receive honour one of another, and seek not the honour that cometh from God only?" (John 5:44; see also Matthew 6:1–4). The sterling test of greatness is not in position or power or public praise.

One of my favorite insights on the sacrificial service of women came from President Spencer W. Kimball: "Among the real heroines in the world who will come into the Church are women who are more concerned with being righteous than with being selfish. These real heroines have true humility, which places a higher value on integrity than on visibility. Remember, it is as wrong to do things just to be seen of women as it is to do things to be seen of men. Great women and men are always more anxious to serve than to have dominion" (*The Teachings of Spencer W. Kimball,* ed. Edward L. Kimball [Salt Lake City: Bookcraft, 1982], 323).

One of the greatest women who ever lived, whose incredible life of service had a far-reaching and profound effect on the whole world, worked humbly among those least likely to offer her public recognition and power. "I get asked my opinions on the role of the Church today, on women's place within it," explained Mother Teresa, "and what the future holds, and I say I don't have time to worry about all these issues—there are too many things to do in my everyday work" (*Mother Teresa, A Simple Path,* comp. Lucinda Vardley [New York: Bantam Books, 1995], 59–60).

Yet, when it comes to church organizations, LDS women have opportunities and responsibilities that far surpass those of their sisters in many other denominations where women do not hold priesthood. Though men preside, women take highly visible roles in Church meetings. Through a revelation to Emma Hale Smith, wife of the Prophet Joseph Smith, the Lord instructed *all* women in the Church ("this is my voice unto all") to "expound scriptures, and to exhort the church, according as it shall be given thee by my Spirit" (D&C 25:16, 7; italics added). This commandment was received at a time when allowing women to speak publicly in church meetings would have been considered heresy by many. Further, "wielding an influence for good, women fill myriad assignments in the Church," explain Barbara B. Smith and Shirley W. Thomas in the *Encyclopedia of Mormonism*.

> They preside over, direct, and staff the organizations for women (Relief Society), young women (Young Women), and children (Primary) at ward, stake, and general levels; they teach doctrinal study classes for adults, youth, and children; they direct choirs and dramatic productions; they officiate in temple ceremonies; they serve as members of welfare committees at all levels of the Church; and they organize cultural and recreational events in which all members participate. ("Women, Roles of," in *Encyclopedia of Mormonism*, 4 vols., ed. Daniel H. Ludlow [New York: Macmillan, 1992], 4:1576)

Consider also this statement from President J. Reuben Clark Jr.:

In all that relates to the supplying of clothing, the preparation and preservation of foodstuffs, the nursing of the sick, the burial of the dead, in all that relates to the infinities of kindly attention and sympathy, in all that relates even remotely to the love and ritual of motherhood, the Women's Relief Society carry the burden. The bishop is the father of his ward; the Relief Society is the mother. The Church Welfare Plan could not be carried on without them; it serves in greatest measure where they are most active. They establish sewing and cooking centers, they help with making budgets, they encourage the heavily burdened and despondent, they hold up the hands of the faint-hearted, they sweep despair out of the hearts of the distressed, they plant hope and faith and righteousness in every household. (*Messages of the First Presidency,* 6 vols., James R. Clark, comp. [Salt Lake City: Bookcraft, 1965–75], 6:77)

The priesthood brethren will readily admit that they would be lost without the sisters in this Church. However, I don't want to imply that men need women any more than women need men. Who can estimate the impact for good in a woman's life of faithful, righteous, noble priesthood leaders? The complementary roles of men and women are described further in the *Encyclopedia of Mormonism:*

The companionship role is the one most often identified for women in the Church. Adam "began to till the earth," and "Eve, also, his wife, did labor with him" (Moses 5:1). President Spencer W. Kimball pointed out that women are "full partners" with men (Kimball, 42). This companionship is not limited to the husband and wife partnership but includes women serving cooperatively with men (e.g., Priesthood and Relief Society) to carry out the work of the Church. From the early days, "the women of the Church have voted side by side with the men on all questions submitted to the Church membership for vote, . . . an advanced concept in 1830 when no women and few men voted in any church and few women had political franchise (*History of the Relief Society,* 102)." (Smith and Thomas, "Women, Roles of," *Encyclopedia of Mormonism,* 4:1576)

Behind the Scenes

Furthermore, consider the great influence women have on the course of the Church because of the daily and hourly influence they have on the brethren who come to leadership positions in the Church. Mothers have the first and most powerful influence on their sons, and wives then become the central focus of their husbands' lives. Wives, mothers, and sisters often serve as unofficial counselors to their husbands, sons, and brothers who exercise priesthood and serve in Church government. Inspired women have thus affected the Church in times past and will continue to do so in the future.

The effect of a great woman's influence was even recognized in ancient biblical times, as shown in the well-known tribute to a virtuous woman that is found in Proverbs, chapter 31. Because of her righteousness and her support, "her husband is known in the gates, when he sitteth among the elders of the land." (In ancient times the leaders and respected men of the city would meet and converse together at the gates of the city wall.) In the Book of Mormon we learn of the well-trained stripling warriors who helped save the Nephite nation and church from destruction because they "had been taught by their mothers, that if they did not doubt, God would deliver them" (Alma 56:47). Mary, the sister of Martha, was so in tune with the Spirit that, whether or not she fully recognized the impending death of her Savior, she was inspired to save some expensive ointment of spikenard to anoint "aforehand . . . [Christ's] body to the burying." This act must have been evidence of remarkable sensitivity and greatness of soul, because the Lord went on to praise her and proclaim, "Wheresoever this gospel shall be preached throughout the whole world, this also that she hath done shall be spoken of for a memorial of her" (Mark 14:8–9). Mary, the mother of Christ, and other women stood by Jesus until the end of his life as he hung on the cross and consummated his atonement.

So central is the equality of all humankind to Christ's message that during his earthly ministry

Christ openly rejected cultural proscriptions that relegated women to an inferior spiritual and political status. He recognized women's spirits and intellects; he taught them directly (Luke 10:38–42); he identified himself as the Messiah to a woman, the first such affirmation recorded in the New Testament (John 4:26); he healed women (Matt. 15:22–28) and raised a woman from the dead (Luke 8:49–56). After his resurrection, he appeared first to a woman, whom he asked to tell his apostles of the glorious event (John 20:11–18), although according to Jewish law women were not considered competent as legal witnesses. (Mary Stovall Richards, "Feminism," in *Encyclopedia of Mormonism*, 2:507)

Further, the Apostle Paul reminded his dear friend and missionary companion Timothy that he had been inspired by "the unfeigned faith that is in thee, which dwelt first in thy grandmother Lois, and thy mother Eunice" (2 Timothy 1:5). Consider the strength and support of the polished and well-schooled Emma Hale Smith on the young, poorly educated, fledgling Joseph as he struggled to translate the Book of Mormon and reestablish the kingdom of God on earth. Joseph F. Smith, sixth president and prophet of the Church and son of Patriarch Hyrum Smith, was raised by his mother, Mary Fielding Smith, after Hyrum's death when Joseph was only nine years old. Her heroic fortitude in bringing her family across the plains without a husband is legendary. Her prophet son "often

spoke of her as a model of courage and faithfulness"
(Susan Arrington Madsen, "Smith, Mary Fielding," in
Encyclopedia of Mormonism, 3:1359).

Undoubtedly, there are many more unheralded examples as well. I know from my own experience that
when my husband or son has served in a leadership position, I have been able to see some solutions that he could
not, to make helpful suggestions, and to give inspired
counsel, just as he has done for me when I have had my
turn at leadership responsibility. To be influential and of
service, one doesn't need to be "in charge."

Direct and Indirect Leadership

However, women can also have a more direct influence
on the Church itself. Perhaps the woman who historically
exerted the greatest and most direct influence on the
course of the Church was Eliza R. Snow. "By the mid-
1880s Mormon women had achieved with distinction.
Relief Societies, Mutual Improvement Associations, and
Primary Associations had been established throughout the
territory, largely through the efforts of women under the
direction of Eliza R. Snow. Women's efforts in these organizations, in home industry and grain storage, and their
willingness to be trained in skills meeting specific needs
of the growing Kingdom made theirs a contribution in no
way inferior to that of their brethren," wrote Jill Mulvay.
She then provided a few specific examples of the substantial influence of Eliza and her faithful sisters in the
Church. "'Presidentess' Snow told the Brigham City Relief
Society, 'Sometimes I think we can do more than the

brethren.' 'We ladies cannot dictate,' Eliza admitted, but the Prophet Joseph Smith had told the women at that first meeting of the Relief Society in Nauvoo that they might 'provoke the brethren to good works.'" ("Eliza R. Snow and the Woman Question," *BYU Studies,* vol. 16, no. 2 (1976), 256–58).

The same sort of cooperative and complementary influence can and does take place today in the Church from the highest levels on down to the stake and ward organizations. The operations and leadership of the Relief Society can have a profound effect on the spirit of a ward. Righteous, inspired women can wield major influence by counseling with the priesthood.

I have often seen the remarkable results of Relief Society and priesthood leaders counseling together and then applying their respective strengths to a problem or challenge. A dear friend of mine who served as the Relief Society president in our ward many years ago recently related one example. The bishop called her in to let her know that a sister in the ward was being disfellowshipped and that he would be working with her to bring her back into full fellowship. He wanted the Relief Society president to visit her and see what support she could provide in the situation. What my friend found appalled her. The woman had been disciplined for immorality. She had resorted to that because her husband had already been "running around" on her. He had not been a man of great moral standing when she had married him, but, as my friend discerned, she had not been able to attract a man of high quality because she had no homemaking or personal hygiene skills herself. Her home was a disaster, as was her life.

This Relief Society president was able to offer help that would have been awkward for and perhaps beyond the abilities or sensitivities of a priesthood holder. She and her counselors went into the erring sister's home and taught her how to clean and cook and make herself attractive to men with higher standards. They worked diligently with her until she began to catch on. Eventually she met and married a man who provided well for her and set a great example for her children, who eventually served missions and married in the temple.

In another situation, my husband had been assigned to home teach a divorced woman. He asked for permission to take me along as his companion so that she would feel less awkward than if two men had come to her. She was determined to be as self-reliant as possible and so found it very difficult to ask for help when she needed it, but need it she inevitably did. To hide her embarrassment, she would send a note through the mail asking for what she needed. During one visit we could see that she was partic-ularly distraught because of problems she was having with her difficult ex-husband, who seemed determined to make her miserable. As we sought to comfort her, it seemed that there was nothing we could do to help. Sitting there see-ing her distress, I tried to think what I would want or need if I were in her situation. It suddenly came to me that I would want a priesthood blessing to give me strength and comfort, and I offered my husband's services. My husband was quite pleased that I had spoken up because he had not thought of it, and she would never have asked for herself.

Righteous Womanhood

Women can also influence the course of the kingdom by accomplishing some things that priesthood leaders cannot do at all. One thing the priesthood cannot do for the Church is to set an example of righteous, balanced, enhanced womanhood for the women of the world that will draw them to the living waters of the restored gospel. I remember sitting in the chapel listening to the women's conference of 1978 and how my ears perked up as President Spencer W. Kimball prophetically declared that righteous women would cause major Church growth:

> Finally, my dear sisters, may I suggest to you something that has not been said before or at least in quite this way. Much of the major growth that is coming to the Church in the last days will come because many of the good women of the world (in whom there is often such an inner sense of spirituality) will be drawn to the Church in large numbers. This will happen to the degree that the women of the Church reflect righteousness and articulateness in their lives and to the degree that the women of the Church are seen as distinct and different—in happy ways—from the women of the world. (*The Teachings of Spencer W. Kimball*, 322)

As Latter-day Saint women, we have many answers that other women are seeking. All women want to be treated as human beings of equal worth to men, but many see no alternative to the perspective that women cannot become equal without destroying the traditional husband-wife/father-mother relationship. I believe that *most* women in the world actually deeply espouse conventional values and desire to preserve this relationship, especially because its breakdown poses such a huge threat to their children and families. Most women recognize the value of traditional families, especially in the more religious and less sophisticated nations of the world. Most are probably even willing or insistent that their husbands maintain their place as head of the home. Consider the tug-of-war at the United Nations Women's Conference held in Beijing, China, in the summer of 1995. There were women who insisted that the only way to stop the abuse of women and promote full and absolute equality with men was by pressuring world governments to grant their female citizens complete control over their own sexuality, including elective abortions and contraceptives for teenage girls. It was not men who came forward to oppose these ideas, but other women determined to protect their families from these irreligious and socially destructive "remedies." As I watched the conference debates on television, I realized that in the "good news" of the gospel and the exalted role of women which it teaches, we can offer these family-oriented women of the world the wonderful compromise for which they hunger.

"Now let me also say that the women's movement is not the greatest movement on earth today," BYU English professor Elouise M. Bell insightfully asserted in a *BYU Studies* article. She continued:

> The greatest movement on earth today is the movement of that stone cut out of the mountain without hands which is rolling forth, as Daniel foresaw, to fill the earth; that is to say, the spreading of the gospel of Jesus Christ throughout the world. *That* is the greatest movement. But it is my firm belief that the righteous objectives of feminism will help accomplish the goal of building the Kingdom. Elder John A. Widtsoe, of the Council of the Twelve, made a relevant statement. He said, "Women bear joint responsibility with men in establishing the kingdom of God. They have a common destiny, which as free agents they may attain or lose according to their own actions." ("The 'Mormon' Woman, *Relief Society Magazine,* 30 (June–July 1943): 372.) I truly believe that the righteous goals of feminism, the wise goals as opposed to the unwise goals, will help us prepare a generation of women more fit than ever before to bear their joint responsibility in establishing the kingdom of God. ("The Implications of Feminism for BYU," *BYU Studies,* vol. 16, no. 4, 538–39)

Thus, women play a vital and indispensable role in the Church, both in working behind the scenes and in being a very visible light to the world. The priesthood organization of the Church with its emphasis on the equal but different role of women provides an alternative to male oppression on the one hand and the chaos of "every man for himself" (and every woman for herself) on the other. Men and women together, filling their divinely ordained, complementary roles, will help to make the Church an irresistible force for goodness and stability in a wavering and bewildered world. President Gordon B. Hinckley, speaking for all priesthood leaders, expressed his appreciation for the absolutely vital complementary role that women play in the Church.

> And so, my beloved sisters, please know how much we appreciate you. You bring a measure of wholeness to us. You have great strength. With dignity and tremendous ability you carry forward the remarkable programs of the Relief Society, the Young Women, and the Primary. You teach Sunday School. We walk at your side as your companions and your brethren with respect and love, with honor and great admiration. It was the Lord who designated that men in His church should hold the priesthood. It was He who has given you your capabilities to round out this great and marvelous organization, which is the Church and kingdom of God. I bear testimony before the entire world of your worth, of your grace and goodness, of your remarkable abilities and tremendous contributions, and invoke the blessings of heaven upon you. ("Women of the Church," *Ensign*, November 1996, 70)

Free from Unrighteous Dominion

6

It is probable that throughout most of history, most women in most of the world have been treated like children, second-class citizens, or even property. The restoration of the gospel in the last days has given us the enlightenment to put a stop to this, but without disrupting the divinely ordained family structure. Modern scripture reveals to us the equality of men and women and that "such equality of women and men is based on the celestial model of heavenly parents, both Father and Mother, who share 'all power' and have 'all things . . . subject unto them' (D&C 132:20) and who invite their children to emulate their example of perfect love and unity and become as they are. Mormons are taught that righteous power, held by heavenly parents and shared with their children, is never coercive but is characterized 'by persuasion, by long-suffering, by gentleness and meekness, and by love unfeigned' (D&C 121:41)" (Mary Stovall Richards,

"Feminism," in *Encyclopedia of Mormonism,* 4 vols., ed. Daniel H. Ludlow [New York: Macmillan, 1992], 2:507).

Instead of espousing the misguided notion that overthrowing the established patriarchal order of the Church will make us free from "evil dominance" by men, we must work within the system to attain its grand promised blessings. This is the only system that will ever truly give us power and make us free. For this reason, I want to advocate that women learn how to deal with unrighteous dominion, which undeniably exists, not by freeing themselves from men or contending with them, but by righteously asserting their own equality, divine value, and God-given agency.

When my husband, Brent, and I were first married, we adopted the husband/wife roles we thought we had seen our parents model. This *seemed* to us to be according to the patriarchal order set forth by the Church. Brent was the head of the family, and because I wanted to be what I thought was a good wife, I would willingly submit to his decisions, right or wrong, democratic or autocratic. He did the so-called men's work—earning a living, keeping up the car, yard, and home repairs—and I took care of housework, tended to the children's needs, and supported him in his Church callings, what some would call women's work. We more or less followed this pattern (I not always cheerfully) for about three years. When I was not submitting willingly, Brent could dutifully remind me that I wasn't being a good wife. We thought that was what Brent was supposed to do.

However, after three and a half years and the birth of

our third child, I felt a deep resentment beginning to build. This patriarchal order, as we perceived it, didn't feel very good to me. Brent was gone at work all day and then spent three nights a week playing basketball, and I could either drag three rowdy little rugrats to his games or stay home with them alone, where I had already been all day long. His job was usually finished by 5:00 P.M. when he came home from work, but I was on the job twenty-four hours a day sometimes. We were too poor to afford a baby-sitter except when we went out together, and I felt I could ask Brent to watch the children only if I went grocery shopping, to the doctor, or on some other unavoidable errand.

Pretty soon, the resentment inside me became anger, and the anger became desperation that all spilled over one day. I ran out the door and to my bishop's house. He listened carefully and was kind, but I could tell he didn't fully understand because he also thought that was the role I was supposed to play. When he later spoke to my husband about the problem, he suggested that Brent tell me to "stop complaining." Painful as that was, I don't blame that bishop or my husband, either. We were all playing according to what we *mis*understood the rules to be.

Once I expressed myself and helped my husband to understand the injustice of the whole situation, he was willing to change. Actually, we both had to change. Because of the overwhelming responsibility of having three small children and no extended family anywhere near us, we had to become a team and work together. That was only the beginning of a long and as yet unfinished process of learning what marriage and family life in the patriarchal order are all about.

Over the years I have witnessed many other marriages and families that have fallen prey to the same misunderstandings about patriarchal rule that plagued our partnership. Some of those marriages have since ended in divorce and left women and children with bitter feelings toward men, the priesthood, the patriarchal order, and the Church in general. Some couples have stayed together without addressing the issues, suppressing the pain, which inevitably foments other problems such as strained relationships or emotional and physical illness. Other couples and families continue to struggle on in the learning process, making necessary adjustments as we did.

For the most severe cases of misuse of the patriarchal right to preside, usually referred to as *unrighteous dominion,* there is absolutely no justification. Physical abuse and flagrant verbal and emotional abuse are not only the result of serious sin but are grave sins in their own right. But in the case of most families, the family member is not aware that some of his or her behavior could actually be considered unrighteous dominion. People often don't realize how their actions affect others. Those involved in such a family situation may have anything from a vague feeling to an almost overpowering assurance that something does not feel right.

It needs to be made clear that women as well as men can exercise unrighteous dominion. In fact, anyone can. Anytime we attempt to compel or control someone, no matter what the means, we are exercising unrighteous dominion. Being fallen, selfish creatures, we all learn to do whatever works for us in order to get what we want or need, sometimes without even realizing it. We may not recognize the toes we stomp on or the feelings we hurt along the way.

The tantrums we throw as children are only the beginning. As we get older, our tactics are usually more sophisticated and subtle, and we are often not conscious of deliberately using them (physical abusers still throw tantrums). As Elder H. Burke Peterson explained in an *Ensign* article:

> Exercising unrighteous dominion can follow many patterns. It may be relatively mild when expressed as criticism, anger, or feelings of severe frustration. [Though these can also leave deep and discouraging wounds.] In more extreme cases, however, unrighteous dominion may emerge as verbal, physical, or emotional abuse. Unfortunately, in its less obvious forms, unrighteous dominion is often either ignored or not recognized as such. . . . By acknowledging and setting right these less-obvious forms of unsuitable behavior, perhaps we may help prevent the more extreme behaviors that can grow out of them. ("Unrighteous Dominion," *Ensign*, July 1989, 7)

Elder Peterson also gave some very helpful and incisive examples of the many faces of unrighteous dominion. One husband worked constantly to give his wife all the material possessions she could want. He was seldom home with her, but when he was, he fell into a pattern of demanding perfection from her and criticizing her when she fell short of his expectations. "How can a woman feel she'll ever become what our Heavenly Father expects of her when, no matter how hard she tries, she never pleases her husband?" was this wife's lament. This feeling is common to too many women (and some men as well). Another husband who had served as a temple worker regularly brought home pornographic magazines and videos and then made "inappropriate and offensive demands" of his wife. Other husbands neglect their wives and families because of other priorities. They may be workaholics, sports nuts, TV addicts, or "noncommunicators." They may even be so involved with Church work that they forget that wives and families come first. Elder Peterson also added the examples of a father who "demands compliance with rules he has arbitrarily set [without consulting the family]"—something that would seem acceptable under the worldly misinterpretation of the patriarchal order—and another father who "unwisely used [family home evening] to find fault with family members," giving little recognition or praise (pp. 7–8).

There are as many other ways of exercising unrighteous dominion as there are people. Women have their tactics as well. I have seen women manipulate their husbands and children with saccharin sweetness, pouting, "guilt trips," withheld affection, sickness, and complaining. And then, of course, there is the well-honed tendency of many a woman to nag her family members into compliance. Any of us may be guilty of trying to intimidate or manipulate others into giving us what we think we want or need to survive. The Lord has revealed that men use their priesthood (and women their influence) unlawfully when they "undertake to cover [their] sins, or to gratify [their] pride, [their] vain ambition, or to exercise control or dominion or compulsion upon the souls of the children of men, in any degree of unrighteousness" (D&C 121:37).

The first step toward correcting any problem is to recognize it. As mentioned, the more extreme forms of unrighteous dominion—physical and sexual abuse—are easily recognized, though not easily acknowledged. These abusers must be dealt with by priesthood authorities and, in some cases, law enforcement. *No woman is expected to put up with physical or sexual abuse to any degree, no matter how much she loves her husband or how high his position in the Church.* She is not doing herself, him, or their children any favors by covering up for him. Seeking to save face by hiding the problem from the world is a sin in itself. His salvation is in jeopardy, and as his equal partner, she has a responsibility to do every righteous thing in her power to get help for him to end such unrighteous behavior. If one priesthood leader does not seem to understand, she should go to the next one up in the line of authority until she gets the help she needs. In an October 1996 general conference address broadcast around the world, President Gordon B. Hinckley unequivocally condemned these and other abuses stemming from fits of anger:

> Unfortunately a few of you may be married to men who are abusive. Some of them put on a fine face before the world during the day and come

home in the evening, set aside their self-discipline, and on the slightest provocation fly into outbursts of anger.

No man who engages in such evil and unbecoming behavior is worthy of the priesthood of God. No man who so conducts himself is worthy of the privileges of the house of the Lord. I regret that there are some men undeserving of the love of their wives and children. There are children who fear their fathers, and wives who fear their husbands. If there be any such men within the hearing of my voice, as a servant of the Lord I rebuke you and call you to repentance. ("Women of the Church," *Ensign*, November 1996, 68)

As previously mentioned, other forms of unrighteous dominion can be more difficult to detect and correct. One sign that you are a victim of unrighteous dominion may be the feeling of resentment that builds up when it seems you have no choice about whether to comply with someone else's requests or demands. You are afraid *not* to give in. You fear the person's criticism, anger, silence, or some other kind of unpleasant response. Many people will resort to these behaviors when their needs are not met, and if such a strategy creates the desired results in you—you give them what they want—they will resort to it again and again, usually without even realizing it. It becomes an established pattern of unrighteous dominion.

Feeling as though you are being treated like a child, with no input in decision making, is another red flag. If you feel that nothing you do will ever be good enough to please the other person, you may be a victim of domination. Always feeling that you are to blame for the other person's problems or unhappiness may signal unrighteous dominion, if that person is fostering or encouraging such feelings. Brookie Peterson, wife of Elder H. Burke Peterson, suggested that "a constant spirit of tension and blame" in the home may indicate a problem with unrighteous dominion on the part of a family member (*A Woman's Hope* [Salt Lake City: Bookcraft, 1991], 87). These are only a few examples. Basically, if you feel you have lost the joy that comes from freedom of choice because of the controlling or intimidating actions of another, you may be a casualty of unrighteous domination. Most situations will take some reflection and analysis under the guiding influence of the Spirit to clarify.

Perhaps the best way to recognize unrighteous dominion in ourselves and others is to compare the leadership or management style in question to the Lord's standard as set forth in section 121 of the Doctrine and Covenants. This remarkable passage offers the perfect pattern for priesthood or any other type of righteous leadership. It is only in exercising this kind of Christlike dominion that we merit the Lord's blessing and power.

> No power or influence can or ought to be maintained by virtue of the priesthood, only by persuasion, by long-suffering, by gentleness and meekness, and by love unfeigned; by kindness, and pure knowledge, which shall greatly enlarge the soul

without hypocrisy, and without guile—Reproving betimes with sharpness, when moved upon by the Holy Ghost; and then showing forth afterwards an increase of love toward him whom thou hast reproved, lest he esteem thee to be his enemy; that he may know that thy faithfulness is stronger than the cords of death. (D&C 121:41–44)

No real power to inspire permanent change in an individual can come through force, fear, or manipulation. These tactics are usually used to gratify our own immediate purposes or needs. They may produce temporary compliance but will never inspire committed followership, produce loyal and loving relationships, or yield enduring effects. As General Robert E. Lee once wrote, "That virtue is worth but little that requires constant watching and removal from temptation" (Emory M. Thomas, *Robert E. Lee, A Biography* [New York: W. W. Norton and Company, 1995], 157). Such tactics are, in essence, useless. Only the use of *persuasion*—teaching, encouraging, inspiring, reasoning, modeling, exemplifying, setting up guidelines, involving others in decision making—will have lasting influence and promote genuine change.

Long-suffering implies that we cannot expect or demand immediate results. The Lord always allows us opportunities to learn and relearn the lessons of life. We should allow the same privilege to others if we would have it ourselves. Real growth rarely comes quickly.

Gentleness and meekness describe the manner in which we should conduct ourselves. They suggest that we avoid anger, yelling, abuse of any kind, pulling rank—"I'm in charge here"—or thinking or acting as if we were superior to those we should be serving, be they spouse, children, ward members, or any others we lead.

Love unfeigned, or true charity—"the pure love of Christ" (Moroni 7:47)—for those we serve is an important key to wielding righteous influence. Feigned love has no lasting influence. I have seen people try to control or influence others by pretending to love them and care about their welfare, but actions eventually speak louder than words, and they are inevitably unmasked in their deception. On the other hand, true charity is the greatest motivation we can employ.

Kindness is essential in leadership, for we must "speak the truth in kindness," or use, as Elder Neal A. Maxwell described it, "candor in the context of love" (*A More Excellent Way* [Salt Lake City: Deseret Book, 1967], 118). We should say whatever we have to say and teach whatever we must teach in the most honest, kind, and upbuilding manner possible. To do this, we must have the guidance of the Holy Spirit. This is where the *pure knowledge* comes into the picture. As we seek to lead righteously, the Holy Ghost will pour out pure knowledge, which will enlarge our souls and fill us with kindness and inspire us in the words we should choose and the actions we should take in behalf of those we serve. Our love for them will be genuine, *without hypocrisy,* and our hearts and actions pure, *without guile.*

Only *when moved upon by the Holy Ghost*—not by frustration or anger—should we reprimand sharply those in our charge. This will certainly be rare. Sharpness, however, does not imply anger or unkindness. It probably means that we no longer persuade, cajole, or exercise infinite patience. It means that the time has come to speak plainly, get directly to the point, and say, "Enough is enough." Elder Peterson equates reproving "with sharpness" to reproving "with clarity, with loving firmness, with serious intent" (*Ensign,* July 1989, 10).

Again, an excellent example is Alma's loving rebuke of his wayward son Corianton in the Book of Mormon. Alma is directed by the Spirit of the Lord, "Command thy children to do good, lest they lead away the hearts of many people to destruction." Therefore, Alma confronts Corianton in plainness, "I command you, my son, in the fear of God, that ye refrain from your iniquities" (Alma 39:12). Alma does not belittle his beloved son, but goes on to counsel and teach him carefully, making sure that he understands the ultimate consequences of his actions and the doctrine of repentance through the atonement of Jesus Christ.

Thus, even though the reproof must cut directly to the point, *showing forth afterwards an increase of love* is just as important to the process, if not more so. We all feel discouraged and even threatened when we are reprimanded. Our self-esteem takes a hit that can tempt us to give up, to think we have failed and nobody loves us, or even to rebel against the reprimand or "kick against the pricks" (D&C 121:38). Showing increased love after a disciplinary action can actually help the person involved overcome these feelings and feel inspired to change—not out of humiliation, but because he or she feels so loved and supported. Those we discipline must know that despite our unhappiness with their mistakes, our love for them and our dedication to their welfare are, as the scripture says, *stronger than death*. They must feel that we would do anything necessary to help them, including giving our lives. "Greater love hath no man than this, that a man lay down his life for his friends" (John 15:13). This is the extent of the love we must have for those we lead and serve if we are truly to represent Christ. This is especially true for patriarchs in the home, who are commanded, "Husbands, love your wives, even as Christ also loved the church, and gave himself for it" (Ephesians 5:25).

Other examples from the scriptures and Church history help clarify the leadership style expected in the kingdom of God (which is almost the complete opposite of the world's view). Christ taught his Apostles that anyone who wanted to be a leader would have to actually be the servant of all those he desired to lead. Leadership in the Lord's kingdom would not be a position of power and control over others, as with the rest of the world. King Benjamin, the Nephite ruler, exemplified this remarkable kind of leadership. At the end of his life, as he gathered his people together and addressed them from a high tower, he reminded them that they should serve each other as he had served them.

> But I am like as yourselves, subject to all manner of infirmities in body and mind; yet I have been chosen by this people, and consecrated by

my father, and was suffered by the hand of the Lord that I should be a ruler and a king over this people; and have been kept and preserved by his matchless power, to serve you with all the might, mind and strength which the Lord hath granted unto me.

I say unto you that as I have been suffered to spend my days in your service, even up to this time, and have not sought gold nor silver nor any manner of riches of you;

Neither have I suffered that ye should be confined in dungeons, nor that ye should make slaves one of another. . . .

And even I, myself, have labored with mine own hands that I might serve you, and that ye should not be laden with taxes, and that there should nothing come upon you which was grievous to be borne. (Mosiah 2:11–14)

The Prophet Joseph Smith also personified and taught a leadership style that consisted of carrying people on his shoulders rather than trampling them beneath his feet. I love the following example, which shows how he applied this to his home life—the real testing ground of true leadership. The account comes from Jesse Crosby, a contemporary of the Prophet.

Some of the home habits of the Prophet—such as building kitchen fires, carrying out ashes, carrying in wood and water, assisting in the care of the children, etc.—were not in accord with my idea of a great man's self-respect. [The Prophet coming to my house carrying a sack of flour he had borrowed] gave me the opportunity to give him some corrective advice which I had desired to do for a long time. I reminded him of every phase of his greatness and called to his mind the multitude of tasks he performed that were too menial for such as he; to fetch and carry flour was too great a humiliation. "Too terrible a humiliation," I repeated, "for you who are the head, and you should not do it."

The Prophet listened quietly to all I had to say, then made his answer in these words: "If there be humiliation in a man's house, who but the head of that house should or could bear that humiliation?"

Sister Crosby was a very hardworking woman, taking much more responsibility in her home than most women take. Thinking to give the Prophet some light on home management, I said to him, "Brother Joseph, my wife does much more hard work than does your wife."

Brother Joseph replied by telling me that if a man cannot learn in this life to appreciate a wife and do his duty by her, in properly taking care of her, he need not expect to be given one in the hereafter.

His words shut my mouth as tight as a clam. I took them as terrible reproof. After that I tried to do better by the good wife I had and tried to lighten her labors. (In *They Knew the Prophet,*

comp. Hyrum L. Andrus and Helen Mae Andrus
[Salt Lake City: Bookcraft, 1974], 145)

No righteous woman would have a problem with
"submitting" to a husband or father who exercised such
benevolent and supportive dominion. This is the only type
of leadership women *or men* are expected to submit to in
the Church. "Wives, submit yourselves unto your own
husbands, as unto the Lord. For the husband is the head
of the wife, even as Christ is the head of the church: and
he is the saviour of the body. Therefore as the church is
subject unto Christ, so let the wives be to their own husbands in every thing" (Ephesians 5:22–24). A patriarch
represents Jesus Christ in his home just as the prophet
represents Christ to the Church and a bishop represents
Christ to his ward. They all should act as Christ would act.
Ideally, submitting to (or perhaps "cooperating with"
would be a better translation) such a leader would merely
be submitting to the will of the Lord as it comes through
him. Unfortunately, husbands and fathers are not perfect,
and neither are wives and daughters, but this is the goal
we are striving toward.

What Can You Do?

"No woman has ever been asked by the Church
authorities to follow her husband into an evil pit," taught
President Spencer W. Kimball. "She is to follow him as he
follows and obeys the Savior of the world, but in deciding
this, she should always be sure she is fair" ("The Blessings
and Responsibilities of Womanhood," *Ensign,* March 1976,

72). Women (and men) are not expected to placidly submit to unrighteous dominion. However, if they are not mindful, they can resort to fighting fire with more fire—using the same unrighteous tactics to try to free themselves from the controlling actions of others. This usually leaves everyone burned out. Marriage and family life become a constant battle. The sin on the head of the wife becomes just as great as the sin upon the head of the patriarch, or vice versa.

In talking with marriage counselors, family therapists, and priesthood leaders, as well as through studying the scriptures, I have put together a few practical suggestions for dealing with unrighteous dominion. There are several things that can be done to improve almost any relationship. However, results are not immediate, and three elements are absolutely essential: faith, patience, and the guiding and sustaining power of the Holy Ghost.

1. Examine your own behavior.

"How wilt thou say to thy brother, Let me pull out the mote out of thine eye; and, behold, a beam is in thine own eye? Thou hypocrite, first cast out the beam out of thine own eye; and then shalt thou see clearly to cast out the mote out of thy brother's eye" (Matthew 7:4–5). Above all, we must first look at ourselves. Are we also exercising unrighteous dominion in some way, either overtly or subtly? Earnestly and honestly looking at ourselves through the lens of the Spirit can help us discern controlling or manipulative behaviors we might not have been aware of. We must be willing to give up our own attempts to control others if we expect those people to allow us the same freedom.

Further, is there something we are doing to provoke unrighteous dominion? Unrighteous dominion is never justified, no matter what *we* do, but that also doesn't excuse our taunting or baiting a person who is prone to it. When I am upset with my husband, I know just what buttons to push to escalate the friction between us. My learning not to push those buttons—hard as that is when I'm angry—has saved us from a lot of useless and bitter quarreling, which always invokes some form of unrighteous dominion on both our parts.

Finally, do we honor and respect the presiding authority in our home as we would the Savior? Does he feel that respect, appreciation, and support? President Stephen L Richards observed:

> We call the ordinance of marriage when performed not only for time but for all eternity a sealing—a sealing of a good woman to a good man of the priesthood, with the express understanding and covenant that the priesthood of the man, if he shall be faithful and live worthy to enjoy it, shall be the supreme authority of the household, and no good woman of our faith begrudges her worthy husband of the priesthood the respect which goes with his high calling. She knows that to build him up in the esteem of their children, and thus make him conscious of the responsibility of leadership is the surest safeguard she can bring to her family in

a world of temptation. The women of the Church rejoice in the priesthood of their husbands. They know that that priesthood is not expressed in autocratic or unrighteous dominion. . . . They know that that priesthood has true virtue within it—the power to bless, the power to heal, the power to counsel, to make peace and harmony prevail. (In Conference Report, April 1958, 95)

Before we are too quick to condemn the men of the Church for unrighteous dominion, we should look at our own part in the equation. As we do, we will probably realize that we have a lot of learning to do as well, and that they will need to be as patient with us as we are with them.

2. *Teach others patiently.*

Loving communication is absolutely essential as we begin to try to correct the problem. We must teach others how to treat us! If they don't know how their behavior affects us, how can we just expect them to know they shouldn't do it? Many women are intuitive and sensitive about the feelings of others, but most men have to be taught. However, women also need to listen; men can teach them a thing or two as well. (I tell my children men and women are *so* different and marriage is *so* hard that if they can make a marriage work, they get to go to the highest degree of the celestial kingdom!)

There are many excellent and helpful books available on communication in marriage and families, so I won't go into that. I readily admit I'm no authority. However, there is an expert tutor to whom we can turn for guidance on communication—the Holy Ghost. If we don't know quite how to get our message across without causing the situation to become worse, we can turn to the Lord in prayer, fast and attend the temple, and endeavor to speak the truth in love by the power of the Holy Ghost. I once read that the genius of communication is to be both totally honest and totally kind at the same time. In fact, it is best to be totally kind first, to express love and gratitude for all that is right about our spouse (at all times, not just before grievance sessions), and then the totally honest part will be more effective.

3. *Hold your ground and exercise faith.*

Even when we speak with the love and guidance of the Holy Spirit, we may not immediately get the reaction we desire. In fact, we may temporarily experience increased unrighteous dominion from someone who is trying to make us go back to the familiar and comfortable patterns. The inspired words of Christ did not always change or calm his hearers. Some were incensed at them. If this happens, the important thing is to continue to quietly assert our needs and feelings *under the influence of the Spirit and with the Lord's assurance that we are justified, not selfish.* We cannot let anger or impatience drive out the influence of the Spirit when we need it most. However, at the same time, we must not back down. We need to continue quietly, firmly, and kindly to assert our feelings, needs, and *love.* It may take several attempts at this effort to communicate before the other person sees that we are serious, that we are not going to give in and accept things the way they were.

It is also important that we teach our loved ones for their own sakes. I have been thankful for my husband's mellowing influence on me. He is helping to smooth off some of my rough edges by drawing the line in what he will tolerate. He doesn't let me get too shrill. I have noticed that in marriages where one partner tends to dominate, the overbearing person also tends to dominate and offend others besides the marriage partner. No one has taught him or her that it is undesirable behavior. Often it is passed on to one or more of the children in the family, and the cycle continues.

4. Maintain power over your own decisions.

Don't fight back, but don't cower or crawl or capitulate either. Have the courage, under the influence of the Spirit, to stand up for yourself and do what you know to be right. Don't allow the dominating behavior to have its intended effect—to control you. You can offer to lovingly meet the person's needs in a more appropriate and agreeable way, but not by giving in to unrighteous demands or treatment. Most people admire those who have enough self-respect to draw the line at what they will and will not tolerate in the way others treat them.

Generally a person will rise to whatever level is expected. If we *let* others have control, they will usually continue to take it. However, if two people are partners in a waltz and one suddenly refuses to go on in the dance, the other will eventually realize it and stop dancing also.

Some women or even men may be so used to giving in

that it is hard for them to stand up for themselves without feeling selfish and guilty. It may help to look to our perfect exemplar, Jesus Christ. Consider an example from the family life of the Savior. In the book of John, we find an account of the brethren of Jesus trying to goad him into doing something he did not choose to do (see John 7:2–10). They wanted him to go to Jerusalem to the Feast of Tabernacles and openly show himself and his works and teachings to the world. They wanted this not because they believed in him and wanted to share his message with others, but because they wanted him openly exposed for the impostor they thought he was. However, Jesus was not moved by their thinly veiled taunt. He had the strength that came from knowing who he was and what was right. Christ never made decisions in response to pressure from others. In this instance, he patiently explained the situation to his brothers—the time for open preaching had not yet come—even though they could not really understand or appreciate his answer. He waited and then went to the festival at a later time of his own choosing, "as it were in secret."

Of course, there were many who attempted on an even more strident level to control the Savior for their own ends. His enemies were continually criticizing, intimidating, accusing, tricking, and persecuting him to get him to back down from the teachings and works that were such a threat to them. They tried all kinds of things to stop him and finally had to resort to treachery and force. (Even then they could have power over him only because he allowed it. Unfortunately, we don't always have that choice in mortality.)

Significantly, Jesus never did allow the actions of others to determine his. He always acted and never reacted. He never lashed out at people in vengeance or defensiveness, but neither was he afraid to stand up for himself and for the truth. He reproved them betimes with sharpness and clarity but never with personal bitterness. Emotionally and spiritually speaking, they just couldn't rattle him. We can achieve the same state of spiritual self-assurance if we are worthy of the companionship of the Holy Ghost. The Holy Ghost will help us discern when we are making selfish, thoughtless, or unreasonable demands and when we are standing up for what is right. Just as Christ could never have fulfilled his mission and done his Father's will if he had allowed others to intimidate him and control his life, neither can we discover the Lord's will for our lives if we let others manipulate us.

5. *Be grateful for sincere efforts, even if they fall short.*

Help the person in question to see how much better the Savior's servant-leadership formula works and how much joy it can bring into your home. Set the example, encourage, compliment, and show appreciation. Employ the Savior's motivating techniques: long-suffering, persuasion, kindness, gentleness, meekness, pure love, and so on. Continue fasting, praying, and attending the temple.

6. *If these efforts fail, involve priesthood leaders.*

When we feel, under the prompting of the Holy Ghost, that we have exercised great patience and done all that we could do and still see no lasting desire to change on the part of the offender, we can reach for outside help. I asked some experts about what a woman can *righteously* and *reasonably* do when a man simply will not change his ways. One family counselor and priesthood leader said to me, "If all else fails, report him to his priesthood leader. That will get his attention. It will let him know that you mean business." Many will change just out of embarrassment, others because of counsel from their leaders. In some cases, more teaching and intervention may be required.

The bottom line is this: Though rebellion against the priesthood is not the answer, women or men do not have to sit back and accept unrighteous dominion in order to be obedient or even Christlike. Just "taking it" is not accounted to us as righteousness if it fosters resentment or bitterness in our hearts and destroys relationships that we have the responsibility to make fit for the celestial realms. Doing nothing is also a choice for which we must be accountable.

7

Free to Use Our Power and Influence

"God bless her gallant heart!" exulted Stanford Smith with tears streaming down his face as he lifted his hat in triumphant salute to Arabella, his wife. He could never have made it without her. In fact, he should not have tried it *with* her, for she was "only" a woman. But Belle had insisted. She had been determined that, together, they could make it. I believe that her story, which follows, is a metaphor for the role and power of women.

Many of the early pioneers arrived in the Salt Lake Valley after the arduous trek from the East only to find out that they were not finished "pioneering" yet. Responding to the call of a prophet of God, they once again packed up their wagons and moved to other frontier areas of the Great Basin to establish additional Mormon settlements. Joseph Stanford Smith was called to settle in the Colorado River basin. He had been one of the most active leaders in helping blaze a trail through a treacherous canyon in southern Utah that became known as Hole-in-the-Rock.

On January 26, 1880, Stanford spent the day helping all the wagons in his company get down through the notch in the rocky canyon. With pulleys and logs tied to the backs as brakes, the wagons were carefully lowered one at a time through the rocky crevice, driven to the banks of the river, and ferried across. When word came that all the wagons were safely down and across the river, Stanford looked for his own wagon—but it was nowhere to be found. It was still up at the top of the canyon.

Stanford was frustrated and angry, but his wife, Arabella, pointed out that the horses were harnessed and everything was packed. They had no choice; they would have to make it on their own. Arabella settled the three young children in a safe area out of the way and told them to wait until the wagon was safely down.

Stanford locked the brakes, checked the team, and tied the old mule to the back axle as a brake. He looked down the crevice—ten feet of loose sand, then a rocky pitch as steep as the roof of a house and barely as wide as the wagon, and below that a frightening rocky chute. It was the drop of 150 feet that scared him to death.

"If we only had a few men to hold back the wagon, we might make it, Belle."

"I'll do the holding back," Belle courageously declared. "I'll hold on to the mule's lines."

Stanford braced his legs hard against the dashboard and started the team down the canyon. "Pull back as hard as you can, Belle," he yelled to his wife. She dug in her heels the best she could. Soon the wagon was speeding down the canyon. The mule was thrown to his haunches, knocked to his side, and dragged. Belle was blinded by the sand that streamed past her. A jagged rock tore her flesh, and she felt a hot pain from hip to heel.

Finally the wagon stopped at the end of the chute. Stanford jumped off the wagon and first noticed the bloodied and bruised and almost lifeless mule, which had been dragged most of the way down. There, holding onto the reins, covered from head to foot with dirt, her leg streaming with blood, was Arabella. She had been dragged down along with the mule—but she wouldn't let go. She had hung on for all she was worth. They had made it down safely (as told by a grandson, Raymond Smith Jones, in David E. Miller, *Hole-in-the-Rock* [Salt Lake City: University of Utah Press, 1966], 111–14).

I have always loved this story of Arabella Smith. There is a part of me that identifies with her courage and her determination and her pulling from behind. Like the women of the Church sometimes do, she stayed behind the scene, not driving or insisting on control but exerting her influence, fulfilling her complementary, balancing, and even "more-than-her-share" role, exercising her power in an indispensable way. Sometimes, as in Belle's case, a woman will be called upon to be tough, gritty, and courageous; countless women have met and continue to meet that challenge valiantly every day. But in most cases, a woman's gentle influence and power will be needed to soften, beautify, and civilize the world around her—not an easy task.

"There are persons so radiant, so genial, so kind, so pleasure-bearing, that you instinctively feel in their presence that they do you good," wrote Henry Ward Beecher, "whose coming into a room is like the bringing of a lamp there." I believe that beautiful thought summarizes, in a general way, the mission of women in the world. Or, as a favorite Relief Society hymn declares:

The errand of angels is given to women;
And this is a gift that, as sisters, we claim:
To do whatsoever is gentle and human,
To cheer and to bless in humanity's name.

("As Sisters in Zion," Hymns, no. 309)

"When the real history of mankind is fully disclosed, will it feature the echoes of gunfire or the shaping sound of lullabies?" asked Elder Neal A. Maxwell rhetorically. "The great armistices made by military men or the peace-making of women in homes and in neighborhoods? Will what happened in cradles and kitchens prove to be more controlling than what happened in congresses? When the surf of the centuries has made the great pyramids so much sand, the everlasting family with still be standing, because it is a celestial institution, formed outside telestial time. The women of God know this" ("The Women of God," *Ensign,* May 1978, 10–11).

Elder Matthew Cowley, a member of the Quorum of the Twelve in the early 1900s, spoke of the "inherent" right and authority women possess because of their calling as "co-creators with God," even if they never actually bear children. "After all, you belong to the great sorority of saviorhood. You may not hold the priesthood. Men are different, men have to have something given to them to make them saviors of men, but not mothers, not women. You are born with an inherent right, an inherent authority, to be the saviors of human souls. You are the co-creators with God of his children. Therefore, it is expected of you by a right divine that you be the saviors and regenerating force in the lives of God's children here upon the earth." (*Matthew Cowley Speaks* [Salt Lake City: Deseret Book, 1954], 109).

Over the years, my eyes have been opened to the reality of my own influence. I have discovered (sometimes the hard way) that there are alternatives to nagging! I have learned that I have power to bring about righteousness and help change the lives of those around me for the better. In fact, if I prepare myself and wait for his help, I can tap into the powers of the Lord.

Faith

A righteous woman can invoke the blessings of heaven upon herself and her loved ones through her faith in Jesus Christ, just as a righteous priesthood holder blesses others through the priesthood of Jesus Christ. Though she cannot perform priesthood ordinances or hold priesthood office, her access to the blessings and powers of God needed in daily life is not diminished in any way.

For example, a simple prayer pronounced with unwavering faith can accomplish a great deal. I have in my family history the following account of my third-great-grandmother, who had been given up for dead at Winter Quarters:

Sister Sallie Norton, . . . was very ill. Everyone had given up hope for her life. A brother, Lane, told them to send for the sisters. . . . Sister Eliza R. Snow, Zina Young, Violet Kimball and Jane Young were called. They knelt around her bed and offered up a prayer to God in her behalf, Sister Eliza R. Snow being mouthpiece. . . . She, Sister Norton, was instantly healed, rose from her bed, and had good health until they reached Utah. (Unpublished manuscript in possession of the author)

Sometimes long-term faith is needed to bring about even more important miracles, such as the softening of a heart or saving of a soul. While such a goal requires infinite patience, I have learned that I must never lose hope and I must always defer to the will of the Lord. Often the Lord has an even greater answer to my prayers than I ever thought of, but it comes in his own time and way. Sometimes things seem to get worse before they get better, and that is where my faith is really tested.

Fortunately, we can do more than just pray and wait. Fasting brings us peace as well as power over our problems. I also can bear witness of the strength that comes from serving in the temple and participating in prayer there. I am amazed at the results of placing a name on the prayer roll under the guidance of the Spirit. I believe we can serve and greatly influence the lives of many people in this way, and they may never even know it!

Inspiration

By cultivating her God-given sensitivity to spiritual feelings, a woman can through faith discern her loved ones' needs and give them inspired direction and protection, just as a man may guide and counsel through priesthood blessings. The fact that the world even has a name for this sensitivity, "woman's intuition," is an indication that it is widely recognized and specialized as a feminine attribute. Many of us could recount experiences wherein our mothers' inspired feelings have guided us away from danger or solved serious problems. This is not to say that men are not likewise inspired, but because of the gift of sensitivity women have been given, along with the assignment they have to nurture God's children and the world in general, women seem to come specially equipped for it.

Women can also use this gift of inspired perception outside the home to help warn others away from the dangers of the world. Elder Boyd K. Packer said, "We need women with the gift of discernment who can view the trends in the world and detect those that, however popular, are shallow or dangerous. We need women who can discern those positions that may not be popular at all, but are right" ("The Relief Society," *Ensign*, November 1978, 8). A woman who can see and perceive clearly when all around her suffer from blurred vision has the power to lead others to safety. She will be a beacon of light in the midst of darkness.

Example

The effect of a woman's example is nowhere more powerful than in the home, where those we live with day in and day out see us at our very best and our very worst. So subtle and yet so profound is the influence of a mother's example that we often find ourselves imitating our mothers, sometimes even when we have been determined not to do so. I have been gone from my mother's home for well over twenty years, and yet I still find myself sounding and acting like my mother, mannerisms and all.

Our children absorb our example into their minds and hearts much as a tree absorbs moisture and nutrients from the earth. No one notices it happening, but the soil is the very lifeblood of the tree and influences the development and beauty of the tree itself and all those trees that spring from it. Indeed, even more sobering than recognizing how I seem to have become a copy of my mother is to see my own example reflected in the behavior and being of my own children. Throughout their teenage years, it seemed that my efforts to teach them had little if any effect. Now that they are young adults, they act, and sound, and even seem to think amazingly like my husband and me. I also see how the behaviors they have learned from me affect those around them. I see how my influence, through my children, is extending throughout the world and will do so for generations to come.

Once again, however, a woman need not have children to see her example profoundly influence the lives of others. She can have great impact upon the women of the

Church as well as the women of the world. The example of a Korean sister, Whang Keun-Ok, had this kind of powerful effect on the lives of several young Korean girls. After joining the Church in 1962, she became the superintendent of Song Jook Orphanage. She always had a smile for the children and knew all of their names and situations. The young girls at the orphanage loved her very much. When they found out she was a "Mormon," they wanted to know about her church. Several of them began taking the discussions, and some were baptized. When the authorities of the church that sponsored the orphanage found out, they informed Sister Whang that she would either have to convert to their faith or find a new job.

In spite of substantial financial challenges, Sister Whang started an orphanage of her own and took with her those girls who had converted to the gospel or were interested in it. There she and her girls started each day with hymn singing, prayer, and scripture study. They rode the bus to church on Sundays and held family home evenings on Mondays. Sister Whang also taught the girls to spread the gospel through music, organizing them into a singing group that helped to bring the Church's name to a greater level of recognition in Korea.

A former mission president of the Seoul mission, speaking of the orphaned girls Sister Whang had raised, surmised: "A couple of them probably wouldn't have survived. The rest of them probably would have ended up as servants or living on the street. Sister Whang truly provided physical salvation for those girls—and gave them the opportunity for spiritual salvation by introducing them to the gospel."

Sister Whang had been determined to place as many of the girls as possible with LDS families. "Of the eighty-four children she brought up over a period of nearly twenty years, thirty-three were adopted into Latter-day Saint homes in the United States. At least twelve have married in the temple, and nine have served full-time missions." Summing up the impact of her example, one of her "daughters" said, "I think of her every day and I use her as a role model. She has taught me that one person can make a difference" ("Whang Keun-Ok: Caring for Korea's Children," *Ensign,* October 1993, 46–49).

Love

"When persons manifest the least kindness and love to me," intoned the Prophet Joseph Smith, "O what power it has over my mind, while the opposite course has a tendency to harrow up all the harsh feelings and depress the human mind" (*Teachings of the Prophet Joseph Smith,* comp. Joseph Fielding Smith [Salt Lake City: Deseret Book, 1938], 240). Love has greater power to effect change in others than force or intimidation. Love *is* a power in and of itself—especially if it is charity, the pure love of Christ. When other people feel our unconditional love, most gain a greater desire to please us. Love, kindness, and forgiveness are even the ultimate weapons we can wield against our enemies. If they are beyond our influence, we are at least freed from hate and fear and all other negative emotions that make us feel powerless. Any woman can manifest this kind of love.

The love of a wife for her husband can be a powerful sustaining influence in his life. Even when he may not be all that she would wish him to be, or all that he should be, faith, prayer, inspiration, example, and love will eventually bring about desired changes in almost every case. "You need not be teazing [nagging] your husbands [fathers, brothers, priesthood leaders, and others] because of their deeds," President Joseph Smith taught the Relief Society sisters, "but let the weight of your innocence, kindness and affection be felt, *which is more mighty than a millstone hung about the neck;* not war, not jangle, not contradiction, or dispute, but meekness, love, purity—these are the things that should magnify you in the eyes of all good men" (*History of The Church of Jesus Christ of Latter-day Saints,* 7 vols., ed. B. H. Roberts [Salt Lake City: The Church of Jesus Christ of Latter-day Saints, 1932–51], 4:605; emphasis added).

The Power of Teaching the Word

We must be as well schooled and prepared as we possibly can to teach those who will come under our influence. The more knowledge we have, especially scriptural background, the more impact our teachings will have, and the better guidance we can give. President Spencer W. Kimball admonished, "We want our sisters to be scholars of the scriptures as well as our men. You need an acquaintanceship with his eternal truths for your own well being, and for the purposes of teaching your own children and all others who come within your influence" ("Privileges and Responsibilities of Sisters," *Ensign,* November 1978, 102).

Just as "the word" is the most powerful force in changing our own lives (see Alma 31:5), it is also the most effective force in influencing others. That is because teaching from the scriptures gives those we instruct a sure foundation on the rock of Christ. In the book of Helaman we learn that a testimony built on outward observances, social convenience, or simply "feel-good" experiences or stories will eventually be unable to stand firm against the constant chipping away of Satan. "And now, my sons, remember, remember that it is upon the rock of our Redeemer, who is Christ, the Son of God, that ye must build your foundation; that when the devil shall send forth his mighty winds, yea, his shafts in the whirlwind, yea, when all his hail and his mighty storm shall beat upon you, it shall have no power over you to drag you down to the gulf of misery and endless wo, because of the rock upon which ye are built, which is a sure foundation, a foundation whereon if men build *they cannot fall"* (Helaman 5:12; emphasis added).

One inspired mother saved her son from serious harm or death by knowing the scriptures, by being in tune with his needs and with the Spirit, and by taking advantage of a teaching moment. In the early days of the Church, missionaries to the southern United States often met with antagonism. Elder Frank Croft, who was serving as a missionary in that area, was dragged into the forest one day by a mob of angry men. They told him to strip to the waist; they were going to tie him to a tree and "lash his back until the blood flowed."

As Elder Croft was removing his shirt, a letter from his mother fell from his pocket. It was a response to a letter he had written to his parents describing the persecutions the missionaries had been enduring. It read, in part:

> My beloved son, you must remember the words of the Savior when He said, "Blessed are they which are persecuted for righteousness' sake: for theirs is the kingdom of heaven;" also "Blessed are ye, when men shall revile you, and persecute you, and shall say all manner of evil against you falsely, for my sake. Rejoice and be exceeding glad: for great is your reward in heaven: for so persecuted they the prophets which were before you." Also remember the Savior upon the cross suffering from the sins of the world when He had uttered these immortal words, "Father, forgive them; for they know not what they do." Surely, my boy, they who are mistreating you Elders know not what they do or they would not do it. Sometime, somewhere, they will understand and then they will regret their action and they will honor you for the glorious work you are doing. So be patient, my son, love those who mistreat you and say all manner of evil against you and the Lord will bless you and magnify you in their eyes and your mission will be gloriously successful.

The man who was leading the pack snatched up the

letter. To Elder Croft's amazement, the hardened look left the man's face as he read the tender words of a mother.

> The man finally arose and said, "'Feller, you must have a wonderful mother. You see, I once had one, too." Then, addressing the other members of the mob, he said, "Men, after reading this Mormon's mother's letter, I just can't go ahead with the job. Maybe we had better let him go." Elder Croft was released and went his way. (As quoted in *Young Women Manual 3* [Salt Lake City: The Church of Jesus Christ of Latter-day Saints, 1994], 20–21)

We must never give up, even if our teaching seems to fall on deaf or rebellious ears. How often I have felt my teaching or suggestions rejected, only to hear my words later echo out of the mouths of my husband or children as if they had thought up the ideas all on their own. (I don't care if I get credit, as long as the teaching sticks!) The older my children get, the more they seem to have heard, though I wouldn't have known it at the time I was trying to teach them. I have found this to be true in teaching all young people. Patience is everything. Sometimes it takes years, even lifetimes, but the effort will not be lost. One day we will see that we have saved souls.

The Errand of Angels

Because of her faith, inspiration, example, opportunities to teach, and her singular love, a woman has a calling and power akin to that of the angels in heaven. Although she must often work without acknowledgment, she has a special relationship with God to aid her in her sacred duties. She is a naturally spiritual being with a unique right to inspiration. She has a subtle but powerful influence for good on those around her. She can make life softer, sweeter, and richer for her fellow human beings. She can inspire her family and others around her to great heights—even to eternal exaltation. "If God made man 'a little lower than the angels' (Ps. 8:5), he must then have made women his very angels," opined Elder William J. Critchlow Jr. (in Conference Report, October 1965, 39). The Prophet Joseph promised the women of the Church, "If you live up to these principles, how great and glorious will be your reward in the celestial kingdom! If you live up to your privileges, the angels cannot be restrained from being your associates" (*History of the Church*, 4:605).

Any woman would be hard-pressed to receive such a noble and affectionate tribute and promise for efforts expended outside the Lord's plan for her. It is my sincere prayer that the women of the Church will come to more fully realize the remarkable, regal capacities that have been bestowed upon them by virtue of their gender. When we learn the source of true power, we will be able to exercise it as a profoundly effective complement to the priesthood in a way that will be a miraculous force for good in the home, the Church, and even the world.

Free to Discover Who We Are

Once we have liberated ourselves from the bondage of Satan's lies, the phony expectations of the world, and the relentless obsessions of our own minds—once we have realized how powerful we truly are as daughters of God— we are free to find out who we really are as individuals and what mission we were sent here to fulfill. I have found that this is a never-ending process of discovery. I must constantly be on guard, for I often cave in to the pressures (some real and some imagined) around me and fall back into old ways of thinking. Satan never gives up on me, but neither does the Lord, and I know who will eventually triumph—if I just keep trying.

Free from the "Work Question"

Let us first address the question that hangs heavily over every mother in this generation. Modern Church leaders have encouraged women to make contributions to society and have always supported the concepts of equal pay and opportunity in the workplace. Their biggest concern about women going to work outside the home has ever been the effect on the family.

The possibilities for a woman's refining influence in the world are breathtaking *as long as* men and women both attend to the home front first. The greatest contribution *any* woman—married or single, working inside or outside the home—can make to the betterment of the world is to help build strong, spiritually and emotionally healthy families. For that matter, a *man's* greatest contribution is likewise to the family, the only foundation of a solid and humane society. We can never save the world unless we save families first.

As Elder Neal A. Maxwell so aptly explained, "The act of deserting home in order to shape society is like thoughtlessly removing crucial fingers from an imperiled dike in order to teach people to swim" ("The Women of God," *Ensign,* May 1978, 10–11). President Brigham Young counseled his own daughter Susa Young Gates, "If you were to become the greatest writer, the most eloquent woman speaker, the most gifted and learned woman of your time, and had neglected your home and children in order to become so; if, when you arise on the morning of the Resurrection Day, you found that your duty as a wife and a mother had been sacrificed in order that you might pursue any other duty, you will find your whole life had been a failure" (Susa Young Gates, "Editor's Department," *Young Woman's Journal,* 5 [June 1894]: 449).

We need to be careful not to succumb to the popular world view that a woman can successfully have both a career and a family without making any sacrifices. One of my husband's students at Brigham Young University was a prime example of this. In a paper prepared for his class, she cited a Church leader's counsel to prepare both for homemaking and for making a living outside the home if necessary, and declared, "I intend to take this counsel to heart." That is commendable and would have been a good way to end her paper, but the proud words that followed had an ominous, self-serving ring to them: "My children and my husband will be taken care of by me, but I will not neglect my own personal ambitions. I want it all. Some say you can't have it all. But I am the exception to the rule. I will have it all!" Surprised and saddened at the dangerous, unbending position she had staked out for herself, my husband penned these words on her paper: "Come talk to me in 10–15 years. I'll really be interested in how you've done along these lines. Remember everything has its cost. I'll be interested in hearing what it cost to obtain it all."

The worst thing about this "cost" my husband referred to is that we often don't realize exactly what it is, and that we are paying or have already paid it, until it is too late. Unwilling to sacrifice or yield complete obedience, we may think we are succeeding in manipulating the Lord into letting us "have it all." However, "be not deceived; God is not mocked: for whatsoever a man [or woman] soweth, that shall he [she] also reap" (Galatians 6:7). It may be only when our children become adults themselves that we finally see the harvest of the seeds we planted and find that we must suffer through the results of our choices for a long time to come, maybe forever.

The only way any woman or man will ever "have it

all" is if she or he submits to the Lord's will. "But seek ye first the kingdom of God, and his righteousness; and *all these things* shall be added unto you" (Matthew 6:33; emphasis added). When we are willing to sacrifice our own immediate desires and gratification, no matter how noble they may be, to first ensure that our families receive our very best effort, those forsaken opportunities will one day be returned to us manyfold. We will, in the Lord's due time—perhaps even in this lifetime—"have it all." Ultimately, if we keep our priorities straight and cling to our covenants, "all that [the] Father hath shall be given unto [us]" (D&C 84:38). Meanwhile, we also reap the benefits of a life made happier and a world made better by a strong family.

Some women are forced by circumstances to work outside the home. Others have made the decision *with the approbation of the Lord* that they should work outside the home. *Those* women need never feel guilty. For those sisters who do not have the peace of mind that comes with the Lord's loving spirit of approval, I beg you to reconsider. The guilt you feel may be beckoning you home to loved ones who desperately need you, though you may not realize it now.

Nevertheless, it is not for us to judge any woman who works. This decision is between her and her Heavenly Father. In an outstanding conference address directed to the women of the Church, President Gordon B. Hinckley confirmed the position of President Ezra Taft Benson before him. "I recognize, as he recognized, that there are some women, it has become very many in fact, who have to work to provide for the needs of their families," he said. "To you I say, do the very best you can." He then went on to caution:

> I hope that if you are employed full-time you are doing it to ensure that basic needs are met and not simply to indulge a taste for an elaborate home, fancy cars, and other luxuries. The greatest job that any mother will ever do will be in nurturing, teaching, lifting, encouraging, and rearing her children in righteousness and truth. None other can adequately take her place.
>
> It is well-nigh impossible to be a full-time homemaker and a full-time employee. I know how some of you struggle with decisions concerning this matter.
>
> I repeat, do the very best you can. You know your circumstances, and I know that you are deeply concerned for the welfare of your children. Each of you has a bishop who will counsel with you and assist you. If you feel you need to speak with an understanding woman, do not hesitate to get in touch with your Relief Society president. ("Women of the Church," *Ensign,* November 1996, 69)

Actually, most women I know, including myself, have had to help augment the family income at some time or another; others desire to keep up skills or have at least some regular diversion from the heavy demands of home life for a few hours a week. Fortunately, today there are many options for women. Knowing that the economy may require more than one income to support a family, I have encouraged my own daughters to develop skills or prepare for careers wherein they can (1) receive high pay and benefits for a minimal amount of work, (2) work part time, (3) work at home, and/or (4) alternate work schedules with their husbands.

As the First Presidency declared in "The Family: A Proclamation to the World": "Mothers are primarily responsible for the nurture of their children. In these sacred responsibilities, fathers and mothers are obligated to help one another as equal partners. Disability, death, or other circumstances may necessitate individual adaptation. Extended families should lend support when needed" (*Ensign,* November 1995, 102).

I do not have all of the answers for every woman in every situation, but I do know that "with God all things are possible" (Matthew 19:26) when we have faith and a determination to do the Lord's will at all costs. If a woman has prayerfully and humbly made a decision to work and it is acceptable to the Lord, he will bless her in one way or another. The same holds true with a woman who wants to be at home.

A close friend of my daughter's, who made a fabulous salary working in the computer industry, became pregnant and wanted to stay home with her baby. The family probably could have squeaked by on the husband's income, but it seemed crazy to give up her high-paying job, though she was willing to do that if necessary. However, she made it a matter of sincere prayer and fasting. When she went to her

employer with her dilemma, the company, which wanted
to keep her, made arrangements for her to work from
home for the same salary. In my own life, I have found that
because my husband and I made the decision that I should
stay at home with our children, when we have been in
need financially, I have been able to go "boldly [with con-
fidence] unto the throne of grace . . . and find grace to
help in time of need" (Hebrews 4:16). Thus, I know this:
If we do his will, God will *always* open up a way.

Free to Soar

Meanwhile, if you are among those women who don't
currently have to answer the urgent claims of family life,
you can make transcendent contributions to the Church
and the world. Although most of us who have heavy family obligations would not trade places with you, in some
ways we envy the freedom you enjoy and pray that you
will use it well to make the world a better place. Whereas
my influence on the world will be heavily concentrated on
a few—my posterity—yours, though perhaps less intense,
can have a much wider reach.

"Do not give up hope. And do not give up trying,"
President Gordon B. Hinckley counseled single members
of the Church concerning marriage. (His counsel applies
aptly to childless women as well.)

> But do give up being obsessed with it. The
> chances are that if you forget about it and become
> anxiously engaged in other activities, the prospects
> will brighten immeasurably. I believe that for most

of us the best medicine for loneliness is work, service in behalf of others. I do not minimize your problems, but I do not hesitate to say that there are many others whose problems are more serious than are yours. Reach out to serve them, to help them, to encourage them. There are so many boys and girls who fail in school for want of a little personal attention and encouragement. There are so many elderly people who live in misery and loneliness and fear for whom a simple conversation would bring a measure of hope and happiness. ("Women of the Church," *Ensign*, November 1996, 68)

These suggestions are only the beginning. There are many people in this world who desperately need mothering! They need your gentle, compassionate touch. They need the hope and guidance that you can give. They need the softening, civilizing presence of a righteous woman in their lives.

When I think of those mothering traits, I think of my younger sister, who, despite many fertility treatments, was not able to have children of her own. It was very painful for her, but she did not become bitter or self-absorbed in pity, but immediately began adoption procedures for the most eligible baby she could find, a little boy from India. She has turned her own difficult trial into a blessing for another, as do thousands of adoptive mothers in the world.

Yet even childless women must be very prayerful; not

all will find their calling in adopting children. Sister Ardeth Greene Kapp, former general Young Women president, was not able to have children but became an effective instrument in the Lord's hands in other ways and has had a lasting influence on the young women of the Church—her "daughters." Women whose families are raised and those who volunteer some of their time outside their homes can also perform many desperately needed services.

Furthermore, just imagine the possibilities of a social, commercial, and political world tempered by the gentle and compassionate hand of woman. Today, the fields of endeavor open to women have become almost limitless. Women can help to foster a more understanding and egalitarian atmosphere, not only through volunteer work and helping professions but also in government, business, and politics. In *Talking from 9 to 5: How Women's and Men's Conversational Styles Affect Who Gets Heard, Who Gets Credit, and What Gets Done at Work* (New York: William Morrow and Company, Inc., 1994), Dr. Deborah Tannen details the results of studies that repeatedly found the same *general* trends among members of the same sex. "Conversational rituals common among men often involve using opposition such as banter, joking, teasing, and playful put-downs, and expending effort to avoid the one-down [inferior] position in the interaction." On the other hand, Dr. Tannen found that "conversational rituals common among women are often ways of maintaining an appearance of equality [even with subordinates], taking into account the effect of the exchange on the other person, and expending effort to downplay the speakers' authority so they can get the job done without flexing their muscles in an obvious way" (p. 23). "The rituals of apologizing, softening criticism, and thanking can be used by women or men," she noted. "But they are more often found in the speech of women" (pp. 56–57). A comment Tannen recorded about one woman's style was representative of women in general: "You have such a gentle way of bringing about radical change that people don't realize what's happening—or don't get threatened by it" (p. 41).

Tannen's work confirms that this gentler communication style of women creates a sacrificial role at work similar to the one we talked about earlier in the home and church. "The kinds of things they were doing, like quietly coming up with the ideas that influenced their groups and helping those around them to do their best, were not easily observed in the way that giving an impressive presentation is evident to all" (p. 136). Because of this, however, women tend to be passed over for promotions and raises by those who value a more self-promoting and aggressive style. Admittedly, in the workplace this is not fair, and therefore many women try to adopt the more noticeable speech and behavior patterns of men in order to get the recognition they deserve. What a shame it would be to lose the balancing, complementary, civilizing touch of femininity in the public arena! Deborah Tannen herself does not advocate that women try to be men—or that men try to be women, for that matter—but that they learn to understand the differences in each other's styles and capitalize on them. Business, government, and the world in general can benefit from a healthy blend of both communication styles.

The Church has not and probably never will publish a list of jobs it would consider off-limits to women. On the contrary, it has always encouraged women to fulfill their potential within the framework of gospel teachings and the will of the Lord. As mentioned previously, from the very beginnings of the Church, Joseph Smith and Brigham Young encouraged women to be more than wives, mothers, and housekeepers. Women were often supported financially in their efforts to become trained and educated for various professions, including all branches of business, art, and medicine. Thus, Latter-day Saint women have a long history and a strong precedent of being progressive, capable, educated, contributing members of society, serving both in and outside of their homes. Women of the Church today have the obligation to carry on this tradition to the best of their ability and according to the guidance of the Lord.

Above all, no matter what our situation in life, we can show our sisters around the world that the family system ordained by God really works and is the greatest hope for society. We can labor side by side with men to show the world the value of putting family first, of honoring and sustaining noble manhood and womanhood and the sacred relationship between the two. We can influence the world to respect and honor women without having to reinvent them. President Spencer W. Kimball insightfully proclaimed that it is an especially noble calling to be a righteous woman in the last days. "The righteous woman's strength and influence today can be tenfold what it might be in more tranquil times," he declared ("Privileges and Responsibilities of Sisters," *Ensign,* November 1978, 103).

Therefore, once *all* women (and men) have given their sincere best to their families, there is no limit to the profound and lasting contributions they can make to the world. "Therefore, hold up your light that it may shine unto the world," Jesus Christ commanded the Nephites. "Behold I am the light which ye shall hold up—that which ye have seen me do" (3 Nephi 18:24). Although we will not convert every person to the gospel and bring all directly into the brilliant light of Christ, perhaps if we hold that light up high enough, a few of its warming rays will scatter over the world and make the way a little less cold and dark for others. Wherever we serve outside the home and Church—whether at work or through community service—we have the "right stuff" in the gospel of Jesus Christ to make a difference and to lead the way. After Brigham Young cautioned his daughter Susa against failing as a wife and mother, he added these words of encouragement, which apply to all women: "If, in addition to your wifely and motherly duties, you can pursue one or more fields of public labor; in fact, all the good that you can accomplish publicly or privately, in addition to your home duties, will be so much added to your eternal crown" (Gates, "Editor's Department," 449).

Catch the Vision!

As I said in the first chapter of this book, I believe we are on the verge of a new era in the Church and that, as

President Kimball prophesied, women will play an ever greater role in the forward progress of the Lord's kingdom. I add my amen to Elouise Bell's assertion that the righteous goals of the women's movement, combined with the power of the restored gospel, have given us more freedom to be a positive influence and power in the world than ever before. I have taught my daughters, and I believe we have to face the fact, that more and more women in the Church will remain single. Further, because of advances in health care, women will become more productive than ever in their later years when their heavy family responsibilities are completed. Technological advances have even provided extra time and adaptability to women who stay at home to raise families. Though women do not take the reigns of priesthood leadership in the Church, there is no such limitation upon them in the world. The possibilities are endless, and we cannot set our sights too high if our motives are righteous and we are in harmony with God's will. I believe he will use us, his angels on earth, to accomplish miracles.

However, this will only happen to the extent that we rise to the stature God has carved out for us. Just as the women's movement has urged women to seek greater education in order to take advantage of greater opportunities, we must actively seek greater education in the truths of the gospel and the truth of God's will for us as individuals in order to reach our spiritual potential.

Just as a soldier arms and prepares himself for battle and then reports for orders, we must arm ourselves with the word of God and the sword of truth and right. We must become well versed in the scriptures and doctrines of the kingdom and prepare our hearts to receive and do his will, whatever it may be or wherever it may lead.

Just as teammates on a winning team work together and back each other up, even though each must play a different position, we must form a supportive network of sisters that allows each individual woman to be her unique self and yet part of a winning team.

Just as pioneer women worked alongside their husbands, brothers, fathers, and sons to bear the heavy burdens of the arduous trek to Zion, we must determine to shoulder an even greater load in our spiritually treacherous journey to a spiritual Zion. Just as these women had to put aside their squeamishness and the niceties of their lives for the rugged, unsanitary life of the frontier, we must push aside our time-wasting oversensitivity and self-indulgent insecurities for the higher good of all. Just as these early Saints followed Brigham Young for a thousand miles through difficult, unknown terrain, we must not quibble with the sound teachings of a modern prophet who is leading us by his prophetic vision through a modern-day maze of evil.

We cannot be the first generation of Latter-day Saint women to fail or even fall a little short of our foreordained missions. Surely, like all our righteous sisters before us, we have the courage to rise to our calling! After all, regardless of our circumstances in life, we all possess the same marvelous innate powers and possibilities. "Rejoice greatly, O daughter of Zion"! (Zechariah 9:9). Nothing is beyond our reach, for, not just figuratively but literally and in truth, we are *all* daughters of God!

Index

Leadership, righteous, 97–101, 104; examples of, 101–3
Lee, Robert E., 98
Lion dogs, 55
Longfellow, Henry Wadsworth, 43
Long-suffering, 98
Love, 32–33, 41–42, 99, 100–101, 122–23
Lyman, Francis M., 51

Manipulation, 94, 98
Marriage: author's, 17–18; Corrie ten Boom on, 19–20; as partnership, 50–51; unity in, 52–53, 66, 70–71; misunderstandings about roles in, 90–92; difficulty of, 107; love in, 123
Martha, 24–26, 30, 80
Mary, 24–26, 30, 80
Maxwell, Neal A., 6, 99, 116, 129
McConkie, Bruce R., 70
Meekness, 98–99
Men: women equal to, 48–49, 89; called to preside over women, 49–52, 104; complementary nature of women and, 53–55, 63; and women partners in family, 63–66; influence of women on, 68–70, 72–73, 79–82; priesthood motivates, 75, 116–17; and women in Church, 78–79; communication styles of women and, 136–38
Millet, Robert L., 50–51, 69–70
Missionary, persecuted, 124–26
Modesty, lesson on, 28
"Molly Mormon," 10
Mormon Tabernacle Choir, 40
Mother in Heaven, 2, 60, 89
Mother Teresa, 76
Motherhood: of all women, 20–22, 135–36; priesthood and, 54, 64; sacrifice and, 58–59; influence of, 116–17, 120; and

teaching scriptures, 123–26; and working outside home, 128–34
Mulvay, Jill C., 52, 82

Nagging, 94, 117, 123
Neglect, 94
Nerve endings, women's role compared to, 68–69
Norton, Sallie, 117–18

O Divine Redeemer, 40
"O My Father," 60
Oaks, Dallin H., 51
Obsession with self, 9, 40
Orphanage in Korea, 121–22
Overdoing details, 28–30
Oxford English Dictionary, 48

Pacific Ocean, searching for, 67–68
Packer, Boyd K., 27, 30, 39, 119
Patriarchal order, 50–51; misunderstandings about, 90–92. *See also* Priesthood
"Patty Perfect," 10
Paul, Apostle, 15–17, 41, 70, 81
Peace, 42–43
Persecution, 124–26
Persuasion, 98
Peter, 35–36, 39
Peterson, Brookie, 97
Peterson, H. Burke, 93–94, 97, 100
Pioneers, 113–15, 117–18, 141
Pornography, 94
Prayer, 117–18
Premortality, 14–15
Priesthood: concerns about women and, 1–3, 46–47, 57; given to men, 50–54, 75, 88; and women after mortality, 55–56, 60; no need for women to hold, 61–62, 64, 116–17; holders of, should respect women, 63–64; presides righteously in home, 65–66; following leaders in, 67–68, 71–72; women can influence holders

of, 68–70, 72–73, 79–82; women work in partnership with, 78–79, 83–85, 87–88; misunderstandings about role of, 90–92; and abuse, 95–96; pattern for leadership in, 97–101, 104; examples of righteous leadership in, 100–103; respecting, 106–7; and unrighteous dominion, 111–12

Priesthood blessings, 65, 84–85

Primary, 77, 82, 88

Rebekah, 69–70

Relief Society, 77–78, 82–84, 88

Repentance, 35

Reproving others, 99–101

Richards, Stephen L, 106–7

Roberts, B. H., 23

Robinson, Stephen E., 36–38

Roles of women: equally valuable, 15, 17–20, 134–36; and motherhood, 20–22; less visible, 58–61; in workplace, 136–39; no limits to, 140–41

Sacrifice, 58–61

Sarah, 63

Satan, lies of, 6, 8–9, 13

Scott, Richard G., 58–59

Scriptures, 33–34, 123–26, 140–41

Seed analogy, 21

Self-contempt, 6, 8–9

Service, 58–61, 75–76, 101–3, 135. *See also* Charity

Sick child asks for blessing, 64–65

Single women, 17–20, 134–35

Sisters, influence of, 72–73

Smith, Arabella, 113–15

Smith, Barbara B., 1, 77

Smith, Emma Hale, 77, 81

Smith, Hyrum, 81

Smith, Joseph, Jr.: and Emma, 77, 81; on influence of women, 83; service of, at home, 102–3; on love, 122–23; on potential of

women, 127; encouraged women in professions, 138

Smith, Joseph F., 81–82

Smith, Joseph Stanford, 113–15

Smith, Mary Fielding, 81–82

Snow, Eliza R., 52, 82–83, 118

Song Jook Orphanage, 121

Spiritual nature of women, 51, 53–55, 127

Stripling warriors, 80

Success, worldly, 7–8

Talking from 9 to 5: How Women's and Men's Conversational Styles Affect Who Gets Heard, Who Gets Credit, and What Gets Done at Work, 136–37

Talmage, James E., 55–56

Tannen, Deborah, 136–37

Tantrums, 93

Teaching, 27–29, 30–34, 123–26

Teammates, 141

Temple worship, 41, 118; women and, 55, 77

ten Boom, Betsie, 19

ten Boom, Corrie, 19–20

Testimony, 124

Thomas, Shirley W., 77

Thoughts, 39–40

Top, Brent, 36; marriage, 18; ward Christmas party, 29; counselor in stake presidency, 33; book on repentance, 35; women and priesthood, 46; Japanese gardens, 54–55; blessing for sick daughter, 64–65; wife goes to beach, 66–68; wife's influence, 69, 82; blessing for divorced woman, 84–85; misunderstood patriarchal role, 90–92; influence on wife, 109; influence on children, 120; student paper on careers, 130

Top, Janey, 65

Top, Wendy: women and priesthood, 1–2, 46–47; homemaker

label, 3–5; perfect body myth, 8–9; unrealistic expectations and depression, 10–11; dating and marriage, 17–18; ward Christmas party, 29; repentance and Atonement, 35; overcoming negative thoughts, 39–40; Japanese gardens, 54–55; blessing for sick child, 64–65; lost in fog, 66–68; influence on husband, 69, 82; unity in marriage, 70; blessing for divorced woman, 84–85; misunderstood marriage roles, 90–92; husband's mellowing influence, 109; influence on children, 120, 126; working outside home, 132–33; sister adopts child, 135
Truth, 13–14

United Nations Women's Conference, 86
Unity, 15–17, 22–23, 52–53, 66, 70–71
Unrealistic expectations, 6, 8–12
Unrighteous dominion: not part of priesthood, 65; definition of, 66, 92–93; recognizing, 90–92, 96–97; examples of, 93–94; and

abuse, 95–96; overcoming, 97–101, 104–5, 108–11; examples of men who don't exercise, 101–4; and examining own behavior, 105–7; and communication, 107–8; and getting help, 111–12

Voting, 79

Watts, Isaac, 40
Welfare Plan, Church, 78
Whang Keun-Ok, 121–22
"When I Survey the Wondrous Cross," 40
Widtsoe, John A., 53–54, 87
"Wind beneath My Wings, The," 61
Winter Quarters, 117–18
Women's movement, 7, 86–87, 140
Working women: family responsibilities, 128–31; decisions, 131–34; contributions, 136–39

Young, Brigham, 129, 138, 139, 141
Young, Jane, 118
Young Women, 77, 82, 88
Young, Zina, 118